The Gospel of John

The Gospel of John

A Translation from the Greek,
with Devotional Reflections

CHARLES C. COMEY

WIPF & STOCK · Eugene, Oregon

THE GOSPEL OF JOHN
A Translation from the Greek, with Devotional Reflections

Copyright © 2024 Charles C. Comey. All rights reserved. Except for brief quotations in critical publications or reviews, no part of this book may be reproduced in any manner without prior written permission from the publisher. Write: Permissions, Wipf and Stock Publishers, 199 W. 8th Ave., Suite 3, Eugene, OR 97401.

Wipf & Stock
An Imprint of Wipf and Stock Publishers
199 W. 8th Ave., Suite 3
Eugene, OR 97401

www.wipfandstock.com

PAPERBACK ISBN: 978-1-6667-8901-0
HARDCOVER ISBN: 978-1-6667-8902-7
EBOOK ISBN: 978-1-6667-8903-4

Unless otherwise indicated, all scripture quotations herein are from The Holy Bible, English Standard Version® (ESV®) copyright© 2001 by Crossway Bibles, a publishing ministry of Good News Publishers. Used by permission. All rights reserved.

For Judith, my very special one,
And for Joseph, Franklin, and Ian,
our beloved sons.
Ps 119:105

Table of Contents

Preface | *ix*
Acknowledgements | *xiii*
Introduction | *xv*
John Chapter 1 | 1
John Chapter 2 | 16
John Chapter 3 | 22
John Chapter 4 | 29
John Chapter 5 | 36
John Chapter 6 | 44
John Chapter 7 | 56
John Chapter 8 | 62
John Chapter 9 | 69
John Chapter 10 | 74
John Chapter 11 | 80
John Chapter 12 | 87
John Chapter 13 | 93
John Chapter 14 | 99
John Chapter 15 | 104
John Chapter 16 | 109
John Chapter 17 | 114
John Chapter 18 | 119

Table of Contents

John Chapter 19 | 125
John Chapter 20 | 134
John Chapter 21 | 140
Appendix | 145
Bibliography | 151

Preface

THE FOLLOWING IS A devotional translation from the Greek text of the Gospel of John appearing in Barbara Aland, Kurt Aland, Johannes Karavidopoulos, Carlo Martini, and Bruce Metzger, eds., *The Greek New Testament* (D-Stuttgart: Deutsche Bibelgesellschaft, United Bible Societies, 2014) (5th Revised Edition).

I am a follower of Jesus and a late-stage lung cancer survivor. I give thanks and all glory to God for giving me the energy to complete this work, especially during the final days of its completion in August 2022 and winter-spring 2022–23. During this period, I was undergoing several intensive courses of radiation and chemotherapy at Stanford Hospital for multiple reoccurrences of the disease, first diagnosed in the fall of 2019.

A dear friend and fellow survivor told me that cancer is a long, lonely road. The disease taxes the mind and spirit with its stark reminders of mortality and life's deceptive brevity. Throughout my journey, I've found comfort, strength and inspiration from being able to return to John's Gospel (as well as referenced passages in the Hebrew scriptures) each day, and read devotionally in the original Greek and Hebrew as I prepared this translation. I thank the Lord for the precious gift of his Word and this time.

A few introductory notes: the footnotes herein are intended to assist the reader's understanding by providing what are hopefully salient exegetical and theological comments, based on the language and message of the original Greek text, including Old Testament references. In preparing this translation, I have also included devotional reflections at certain points. These are offered as an opening to meditation, reflection, and prayer as the reader considers the reading and listens for the Spirit's leading.

In rendering the translation, I have consulted a range of sources to ensure clarity where questions of usage or alternative forms or readings have arisen in the textual tradition: Ned Stonehouse, et al., eds., *The New*

Preface

International Commentary on the New Testament (Grand Rapids: Eerdmans Publishing Co., 2007) (e-version) ("NICNT"); Bruce Metzger, ed., *A Textual Commentary on the Greek New Testament* (D-Stuttgart: Deutsche Bibelgesellschaft, United Bible Societies, 1996) (2nd ed.) ("Metzger"); Thomas Oden, general ed., *Ancient Christian Commentary on Scripture Updated Version* (Downers Grove, IL: IVP Academic, 2019) (e-version) ("ACCS"); (in limited instances) R.V.G. Tasker, *John* (Leicester: Inter-University Press, 2000) (Tyndale New Testament Commentaries) ("Tasker"); Frederick William Danker, ed., *A Greek-English Lexicon of the New Testament and other Early Christian Literature* (Chicago and London: University of Chicago Press, 2000) ("BDAG"); *The ESV Study Bible* (Wheaton: Crossway Bibles, 2007) and footnotes therein; and Archbishop J.H. Bernard, *A Critical and Exegetical Commentary on the Gospel according to St. John* (New York: Charles Scribner's Sons, 1929), Vols. I and II (The International Critical Commentary, "ICC") ("Bernard"). I have also consulted and drawn from Mathew Poole's *A Commentary on the Holy Bible*, available online at https://www.studylight.org/commentaries/eng/mpc/john-1.html; and Matthew Henry, *Matthew Henry's Commentary on the Whole Bible*, (Grand Rapids: Zondervan, 1961) ("Matthew Henry"). Certain additional references and critical sources are cited in the footnotes.

Regarding certain conventions used herein: First, books of the Bible are abbreviated using conventional abbreviations (e.g., "Matt" for the Gospel of Matthew). References to the English Standard Version of the Bible are denoted with "ESV." Also, when referring to God by name, the terms "Lord" and "[YHWH]" are used to represent the Tetragrammaton, or יְהוָה, the sacred personal Hebrew name of God in Judaism and Christianity. Third, verbs of speech or motion are often written in the present tense in New Testament Greek narrative, known as the "historical present." Consistent with context, I have reflected these verbs in the simple past tense as they would typically appear in English. Fourth, where works are cited without page references in the footnotes, the citation is to an e-version commentary on the scriptural verse referenced. Finally, I've indicated points in the text where a natural pause or break arises in the narrative with an extra line space between consecutive verses.

(A brief aside on commentaries generally: apart from Calvin's *Commentaries on the Psalms* (Grand Rapids: Wm. B. Eerdmans Publishing Company, 1948), generously gifted to me by Pastor Frank Vanderzwan (ret.) of Menlo Church, and Matthew Henry's Commentary, the ICC is one

Preface

of the finest commentary series I know of, in that it combines attention to the *meaning and nuances of the text's original Biblical language(s) (Hebrew, Aramaic and Greek)* with careful exegesis and commentary.)

With that said, the translation that follows and any resulting errors therein are entirely my own.

Acknowledgements

I WOULD LIKE TO thank the following: Pastors Frank Vanderzwan (ret., Menlo Church, Menlo Park, CA), Dennis Folds (ret., Tokyo Baptist Church, Tokyo, Japan), Nate Showalter (ret., Abundant Grace International Fellowship, Shanghai, China) and David Jones and Iron Kim of Grace Presbyterian Church in Palo Alto, CA, for their faithful preaching of God's Word and gifts of mercy and friendship; and Fuller Theological Seminary Affiliate Professor of Christian Ethics Ron Sanders and Sheriene Saadati, for their helpful critical review and editing; my biblical Hebrew teachers Drs. Kyong-Jin Lee, Russell Fuller, Kyoungwon Choi, and Richard McDonald, who helped me so much to read and discover the treasures of the Tanakh in the beauty and power of its original Hebrew text; Dr. Robert Plummer, Professor of Biblical Studies at Southern Seminary, who deepened my knowledge of the New Testament and its nuances in the original Koine Greek through his thought-provoking, faithful teaching online via Daily Dose of Greek[1]; Matthew Horwitz and Sharon Hamrick of St. Patrick's Seminary & University for their kind assistance in locating reference works I've used in preparing this translation; Fuller Theological Seminary and my Fuller professors during my studies for the MAT degree, especially Ron Sanders (Ethics), Daniel Kirk (New Testament), Peter Hintzoglou (Greek and Exegetical Methods), and Susan Phillips, whose Practices of Community course sharpened my understanding of Scripture and the Christian reflective tradition; Prof. Miles Van Pelt of Reformed Theological Seminary, for gracious advice on Biblical language resources; beloved current and former Morrison Foerster partners and colleagues including David Fioccola, Joel Haims, Tim Harris, Bryan Wilson, Bernie Pistillo, Chip Lion and Suzanne Graeser for their friendship and encouragement especially during my cancer treatments; dear family members near and far, my eldest son Joseph for

1. *See* Daily Dose of Greek, "Daily Dose of Greek."

Acknowledgements

his help in preparing the final manuscript of this book, my younger sons Franklin and Ian, and most of all my beautiful and loving wife Judith (Prov. 31:29).

I pray this translation and the accompanying devotional reflections will inspire readers to read the Gospel of John, and all of the Bible, with reference to the original Greek and Hebrew, receiving its convicting and cleansing power to walk faithfully with God, in love and service to others. As John Wesley reminds us with his timeless charge:

> "The main point is, with all and above all,
> Study the Greek and Hebrew Bible, and the love of Christ."[2]

---

2. Quoted in Van Pelt and Pratico, *Graded Reader of Biblical Hebrew*, x.

Introduction

John's Prologue and the Meaning of the Incarnation

The prologue of John's Gospel (1:1–18) begins with a single point of revelation: Christ the Word, *ho logos* (ὁ λόγος) in the Greek.

To understand the idea of "the Word" and its implications, it is helpful to briefly review the Jewish and Hellenistic thought-world of first-century Palestine in which John "the beloved disciple" lived and wrote.

Interestingly, the Greek philosophical and Jewish theological traditions of John's day both pursued the idea of a "divine word:"

> "Λογος is from λεγω, [an] old word in Homer [meaning] to lay by, to collect, to put words side by side, to speak, to express an opinion. Λογος is common for reason as well as speech. [Greek pre-Socratic philosopher] Heraclitus described it as the controlling principle of the universe. The Stoics employed it for the soul of the world, and [Roman emperor and Stoic philosopher] Marcus Aurelius used σπερματικος λογος [literally, 'word of seed', or 'fruitful word'] for the generative principle in nature. The Hebrew [term] *memra* [מימרא, taken from the root אמר/*'mr*, "say, speak"] was used in the Targums[1] for the manifestation of God like the Angel of Jehovah and the Wisdom of God in Pr. 8:23 ... John's standpoint is that of the Old Testament [rather than] that of the Stoics ... [or] even of Philo."[2]

---

1. The Targums are original spoken Aramaic interpretive paraphrases of the Hebrew Bible dating from approximately the first-century AD when the common language in Israel was Aramaic, and biblical Hebrew was used in worship and schooling only. The Targum paraphrases were used as liturgical explanations in the synagogue service. See Bouyer, *Meaning of Sacred Scripture*, 28.

2. Philo of Alexandria (d. 50 AD?) was a Hellenistic Jewish philosopher in the first century AD who utilized allegory in an effort to harmonize the Torah with Greek philosophy.

INTRODUCTION

References to ὁ λόγος in the New Testament include John 1:1,14; Rev. 19:13; and 1 John 1:1 "concerning the Word of life."[3]

In the prologue to his Gospel, John presents the Word, ὁ λόγος, as being not only coexistent with the Father from all eternity in John 1:1, but further as having "become flesh and dwelling among us" in 14:1.

As his Gospel opens, John therefore is teaching us that Jesus, the Word, is the Revealer of God (1:18).[4] In effect, John is carrying forward from Jewish tradition the implicit but never fully articulated idea of God's word constituting and revealing His person to humanity through His creation, covenant and revelation.

Regarding that tradition, nineteenth-century Irish Anglican scholar and Archbishop of Dublin J. H. Bernard writes:

> "The Hebrew Scriptures have much to say about the Divine Voice in creation, the Creative Word (see John 1:3). In the Targums, or paraphrases of the Old Testament, the action of . . . [YHWH] is constantly described as His "Word" (ארמימ), the term *Memra* being sometimes used as of a Person. Thus, the Targum of Onkelos on Gen. 28:21 says that Jacob's covenant was that 'the Word of . . . [YHWH] should be his God' . . .
>
> The idea in the Greek of a Divine λόγος "was widely distributed in the first century. The Hebrew Targums . . . the Wisdom literature of Judaism, . . . Philo; the philosophy of Heraclitus, and that of the later Stoics, all use the idea of the Logos to explain the mysterious relation of God to man.
>
> . . . But the philosophers, whether Hebrew or Greek . . . *had not found it possible to bridge the gulf between God and man.* How can we reconcile Spirit and Matter, the One and the Many, the Infinite and the Finite? It was left for Christian philosophy to proclaim the only solution of these problems, which metaphysics had failed to solve, was *historical.* And the first statement of this is in the

---

"Philo, thinking of the Book of Wisdom and attempting to express his Jewish faith in terms that he derived from the [Greek] philosophers, says that the entire universe as it is apprehended by the mind is the 'idea of ideas,' the very Word of God. Elsewhere he comes a little closer to attributing personhood to the Word, saying that the *logos* was the first-born of God, an intermediary between the divine and the material, as Plato's forms occupied an intermediary position between the ultimate form, that of the Good, and the formed and material creatures of the world. For 'the most foundational being is God, and second is the Word of God.'"

Esolen, *In the Beginning*, 13 (citing Philo's *On the Creation*).

3. Robertson, *Word Pictures*, 5:4.

4. Bernard, *Critical and Exegetical Commentary*, 1:cxlii.

Introduction

Prologue to [John's] Gospel, Καὶ ὁ λόγος σὰρξ ἐγένετο ["the Word became flesh", 1:14]. *The philosophers had said that the Word is the Revealer of God. That is true, for Jesus is the Word."*[5]

Reading John's prologue, we can also see another difference that John draws between Christ the Word and מימרא and ὁ λόγος as conceived in Philo and the Greek philosophical schools, namely its Incarnational nature: "For Greek thought in general the logos, as a participant in the divine order, was by that very fact *distinct* from the material and historical world. *By contrast, for John, the Word is revealed precisely in His 'becoming flesh'.*"[6]

In other words, *because* He is the Son of God and has become flesh, Jesus is the only way from heaven to earth and back again.

Having lived, studied, and worked in China and Taiwan in the 1980s and from 2003–2010, I find it interesting that every Chinese translation of John 1:1 and 14:6 I am familiar with translates "the Word" (ὁ λόγος; *logos*) as 道 (*dao*) or 道路 (*dao lu*), which in English means "path" or "way":

太初有道，道与神同在，道就是神。
这道太初与神同在(1:1)。
耶稣说我就是道路、真理、生命；若不藉着我，没有人能到父那里去(14:8)。

Read within this context, it is striking how from its very opening words Jesus' story as told by John transcends and, in the process, transfigures the wisdom of humanity's greatest ancient cultures, not only the Greek idea of ὁ λόγος, but also the cornerstone of Chinese philosophical tradition embodied in the 道 (*dao*).

(First articulated during the Spring and Autumn and Warring States periods of the Zhou dynasty (1046–256 BC), the concept of the 道 (*dao*) carries multiple interpretations. Most fundamentally, it refers to the transcendent and incessantly imminent 'way' of the cosmos, always present and always emerging as it creates the world.[7]) In the Gospel of John however we discover an entirely different reality beyond the classical philosophical conceptions of ὁ λόγος, or 道. In John's prologue, God the creator reveals Himself personally with the express purpose of saving humanity. The one

---

5. Bernard, *Critical and Exegetical Commentary*, 1:cxxxviii-cxliii (emph. added).
6. Milne, *Message of John*, 32 (emph. added).
7. *See* Stefon, "Dao."

who brings this change about is none other than Jesus the Word, as John and other New Testament witnesses testify:

"**The Word became flesh** and dwelt [literally, tabernacle] among us ... full of grace and truth." 1:14.
Καὶ ὁ λόγος σὰρξ ἐγένετο καὶ ἐσκήνωσεν ἐν ἡμῖν, ... πλήρης χάριτος καὶ ἀληθείας.
道成了肉身,住在我们中间充充满满地有恩典,有真理.

"But Jesus answered them, '**My Father is working until now, and I too am working**" (5:17),
Ὁ δὲ Ἰησοῦς ἀπεκρίνατο αὐτοῖς· ὁ πατήρ μου ἕως ἄρτι ἐργάζεται κἀγὼ ἐργάζομαι·
耶稣就对他们说,**我父作事直到如今,我也作事**.

"For by Him all things were created, in heaven and on earth, visible and invisible ... **all things were created through Him and for Him. And He is before all things, and in Him all things hold together**" (Col. 1:16–17).
ὅτι ἐν αὐτῷ ἐκτίσθη τὰ πάντα ᵀ
  ἐν τοῖς οὐρανοῖς καὶ ἐπὶ τῆς γῆς ...
τὰ πάντα δι᾽ αὐτοῦ καὶ εἰς αὐτὸν ἔκτισται·
καὶ αὐτός ἐστιν πρὸ πάντων
καὶ τὰ πάντα ἐν αὐτῷ συνέστηκεν ...
因为万有都是靠他造的,无论是天上的,
地上的,能看见的,不能看见的.
...一概都是借着他造的,又是为他造的.
他在万有之先,万有也靠他而立.

"And He who was seated on the throne said, '**Behold, I am making all things new.**' Also He said, 'Write this down, for these words are trustworthy and true'" (Rev. 21:5).
Καὶ ⌜εἶπεν ὁ καθήμενος ἐπὶ τῷ θρόνῳ· ἰδοὺ ⌜**καινὰ ποιῶ**⌝ πάντα καὶ λέγει ᵀ· γράψον, ὅτι οὗτοι οἱ λόγοι πιστοὶ καὶ ἀληθινοί ᵀ εἰσιν.
坐宝座的说,**看哪,我将一切都更新了**. 又说,你要写上. 因这些话是可信的,是真实的。

Introduction

In John's prologue then, we learn several fundamental truths about Jesus. John develops these further as continuing themes throughout the rest of his gospel:

- First, as the Word of God, Jesus is one in essence with the Father and the perfect expression of God's person and His redeeming power and love. There is no distinction between God the Father and God the Son, His spoken Word.[8] In the dynamic symphony of the Trinity, the words and deeds of Jesus are the words and deeds of God Himself.[9] Christ coexisted with God in the beginning, is God Himself and is the very agent of the creation described in Gen. 1:1ff:

    *"In the beginning was the Word, and the Word was with God,
    And the Word was God.
    He was in the beginning with God.
    All things were made through Him, and without Him there was not anything made that was made"* (1:1–3).

- Second, Jesus embodies God's life, and His life is our light. The darkness of our souls and in our world is very real, but Jesus' light shines nonetheless. The darkness is powerless to stand against Christ our Redeemer:

    *"In Him was life, and the life was the light of humanity.
    The light shines in the darkness, and the darkness has not overcome it"* (1:4–5).

- Third, Jesus is God's only begotten (not created) Son, and in Him we see God's glory:

    "And the Word became flesh and dwelt among us, and we have seen His glory, glory as of the only begotten from the Father, full of grace and truth" (1:14–15).

---

8. Milne, *Message of John*, 33. Milne notes: "The significance of this opening phrase of John is that the God who speaks in the Old Testament, who entered into covenant with his people Israel, and inspired and moved the prophets, *was none other than the God known in Jesus Christ. God has not changed or evolved. Jesus Christ was always at the heart of God*" (emph. added).

9. Bruce, *Gospel of John*, 31.

Introduction

- Finally, Jesus is the way God chooses to reveal Himself to humanity. Christ is the one of whom the writer of Hebrews says "He is radiance of the glory of God and the essence of His being, bearing all things by the word of His power" (Heb. 1:3), and whom Paul writes in Colossians "For by Him all things were created, in heaven and on earth, visible and invisible…He is before all things, and in Him all things hold together" (Col. 1:16–17).

> *"No one has ever seen God; the only God, who is at the Father's side, He has made Him known" (1:18).*

John's message is that ultimate "wisdom" is to be found not in philosophical concepts like ὁ λόγος or the 道, but in Christ "the Word" through Whom God "spoke" the world into being at the beginning of time. Christ is thus not only the agent of creation but also, incredibly, the Savior of mere humanity.

Think about what this suggests about how highly God values people. Jesus is God's love personified, coming to earth to die that we may live. His power and kingdom never end, and as Messiah He enters human history "full of grace and truth" (1:14b).

Where does John's prologue find you today? Reflect on John 1:1–18, and travel where it leads you.

1

John Chapter 1

VERSES 1-14[1]

1 In the beginning[2] was the Word,
and the Word was with God,
and God was the Word.
2 He was in the beginning with God.
3 All things were made through Him,[3]
and without Him there was not anything made that was made.[4]

---

1. The verses in 1:1–5, 10–18 below are set out in stanza form in order to highlight their character as "The Logos Hymn," written in praise of Christ, the incarnate Word of God. See Bernard, *Exegetical Commentary*, 1:1.

2. John assumes that his readers know their Hebrew scriptures, including the song of creation that begins the Bible:

> John 1:1's opening phrase "'In the beginning' links directly to Genesis 1:1 [and is] ... shorthand for Genesis. 'The Word of God' appears in Genesis chapter 1 as the means whereby God accomplishes His acts of creation: 'God said, "Let there be light"' (so also Gen 1:6, 9, 11, 14, 20, 24, 26). The Word of God is God himself in his creative action" (Milne, *Message of John*, 31).

John's first testimony about Christ the "Word of God" is that Jesus' story is creation's own story. He is not only present at creation but also – as the divine Word – God's expression to call the universe into being.

3. Lit., *were* or *became*.

4. Even the poetic King James Version's rendering of 1:3b (incorporated here) strains to encapsulate the breadth and wonder of creation's beginning as it is expressed here in the Greek.

> "To John the Word is a Personal Divine Agent who cooperated with the Creator in the work of Creation, even Jesus Christ, the Son of the eternal Father" (Bernard, *Exegetical Commentary*, 1:cxl).

4 In Him was life,
and the Life was the Light of men;[5]
5 And the Light shines in the darkness,
and the darkness did not overcome it.[6]
6 There was a man, sent from God, named John;
7 He came to witness so that he might testify concerning the Light, so that all might believe through him.
8 He was not the Light, but [he came] to bear witness concerning the Light.
9 The True Light, who enlightens all people, was coming into the world.
10 He was in the world,
and the world was made through Him,
but the world knew Him not.
11 He came to His own,
but His own did not receive Him.[7]

John affirms "the dependency of all being upon God, upon His divine artistry . . . St. John states, once and for all, as though to destroy in its root this perverse tendency of the human intellect to re-create the world: ALL THINGS were made through Him (namely, the Word, the Logos, of God) and without Him was made NOTHING that was made . . . Nihilism is the denial of this all-encompassing Word through whom the All was made; Christianity is the acceptance, the passionate embrace, the adoration of this Word, and the love for the All which exists through it and for it" (Esolen, *In the Beginning*, xv).

5. These verses call to mind passages in the disciple's letter, specifically in 1 John 1 and 5, regarding the light and life that Jesus brings to the world:

"This is the message we have heard from Him and proclaim to you, that God is light, and in Him is no darkness at all . . . if we walk in the light, as He is in the light, we have fellowship with one another, and the blood of Jesus His Son cleanses us from all sin . . ." (1 John 1:5, 7).

"the darkness is passing away and the true light is already shining . . . Whoever loves his brother abides in the light, and in him there is no cause for stumbling . . ." (1 John 2:8b, 10 [ESV]).

"If we receive the testimony of men, the testimony of God is greater, for this is the testimony of God that He has borne [witnessed to] concerning His Son . . . *And this is the testimony, that God has given us eternal life, and this life is in His Son. Whoever has the Son has life; whoever does not have the Son of God does not have life*" (1 John 5:9, 11–12 [emph. added] [ESV]).

6. No evil can stand against the power of Christ's life and light.

7. Esolen observes that v11 is the fourth time "John says pointedly something was *not*." First, without Jesus, there was nothing made that was made (1:3). Second, the darkness did *not* overcome the God-spoken light shining into it (1:5). Third, even though world itself was made through Christ, it did *not* know Him (1:10). And now, John here testifies that even God's supposedly chosen people Israel do *not* recognize or receive their Messiah. Jesus' own people "do not take hold of him, they do not bring him into

John Chapter 1

12 But whosoever did receive Him,
He gave to them power to become children of God,
to those believing in His Name.
13 These were not of blood nor of the will of the flesh nor from a husband's will,
but were born of God.[8]
14 And the Word became flesh
and dwelt among us,[9]
And we beheld His Glory,
glory as of the only begotten from the Father,
    Full of grace and truth.[10]
15 John testified concerning Him and cried out saying,
    'This is He of whom I said, the One coming after me ranks above me, because He was before me.
16 For from His fullness we all received indeed grace upon grace;

---

their heart and minds" (Esolen, *In the Beginning*, 68). Israel's rejection of the Messiah is precisely Isaiah's lament: "He was despised and rejected by men . . . we esteemed him *not*" (Isa 53:3) (emph. added).

8. In the original Greek text, the verb "born" (literally, "but from God were born") appears as the final word in the verse, as if to emphasize the distinction between earthly and divine (or spiritual) birth. The latter is solely the result of God's sovereignty and mercy. God alone makes possible our spiritual rebirth through the revelation of and atonement provided by Jesus.

9. John writes here against Docetism, a heresy in the early church claiming that Jesus' human form was only an illusion—the argument was because he was divine, he could not have also have been human.

John 4:2–3 explicitly refutes this position: "By this know you the Spirit of God: every spirit that confesses that Jesus Christ has come *in the flesh* is from God, and every spirit that does not confess Jesus is not from God. This is the spirit of the antichrist, which you heard was coming and now is in the world already" (emph. added). Docetism had largely died out by the end of the first millennium AD (See Wikipedia, "Docetism").

10. "Here we have the climax of the Johannine doctrine of Christ as the Word . . . The Logos of philosophy is, John declares, the Jesus of history" (Bernard, *Exegetical Commentary*, 1:19).

Regarding Christ's reprise of creation through his incarnation, Esolen writes:

> "[T]his ultimate condescension of the Word is poetically just and is possible only by God and in God. The redemption is a re-creation, as Saint Paul says, again and again. It is . . . a more radical creation than the first. In the first creation, heaven and earth come into being from the inanity of what was waste and void. In the second creation, Christ comes to dwell within the soul of a creature who, though made in the image of God, has turned with a will toward non-existence [evil]. In the first, there is life where there had been nothing. In the second, there is life where there had been death, the will to death" (Esolen, *In the Beginning*, 90).

17 For the law was given through Moses; grace and truth came through Jesus Christ.

* * *

REFLECTION: GRACE AND TRUTH

I am the quintessential type A. How constantly do I need truth and grace, and how seldom do I admit my need for either!

For much of my life, I was all about control, and *mine* was the kingdom. But dealing with cancer has taught me that I'm not in control. A daily lesson I receive is to remember to recognize God's grace and truth, which includes his sovereignty in all things. Whether in sickness or in health, my life is in his hands.

Grace or *χάρις* in the Greek corresponds to the idea in Hebrew of חֶסֶד, which refers to God's faithfulness, kindness, and mercy. For the Christian, grace begins with and is only possible through Jesus' atonement.

In John 1:17, John teaches us that notwithstanding the law, Jesus is the new mediator of God's grace to humanity:

> The words of God, the ten commandments, were engraved in stone on Sinai for Moses as the expression of God's kindness in the old covenant. The Word of God is now engraved in the flesh of Jesus as the embodiment of God's kindness in the new covenant. God would not let Moses see Him in the Old Testament [as John writes in v18, "no one has ever seen God"] now the Son who has known Him for all eternity reveals Him. The Gospel is the story of that revelation."[11]

Only when we show to others, however, is grace complete. We bear with, forgive, and serve others, in a measure not possible by our own effort. A hard lesson for me is showing grace to and forgiving myself, for past mistakes or things I feel should have done but didn't. That latter type of regret for me has been the hardest to let go of. But by grace it's possible to forgive yourself, and by grace to live honestly as a witness and messenger of Jesus.

Truth, on the other hand, frees and confronts. As with grace, we desperately need truth in our lives. We live in an age of deception but ironically are also the biggest perpetrators of deception against ourselves. Dostoevsky observed that "Lying to ourselves is more ingrained than lying to others." This is why Jesus said, "I AM the Truth" (and the Way and the Life).

---

11. Brown, *According to John*, 24.

Without Christ, I cannot confront the truth of my sin and desperate need for restoration with God.

Later in John's narrative, Jesus repeats the testimony that the law is given through Moses ("Did not Moses give you the law? But none among you does the law" (John 7:19).

The point here in John 1:17 is that Moses may have given the law, but Christ himself is the ultimate source of grace and truth.[12] It's not that the Mosaic law isn't true, so far as it goes, but rather that the truth of Christ frees the believer from bondage to the law. Put another way, the law was given through Moses, but it alone can't save us.

However, as the perfect "Lamb of God" (1:29) Jesus has *already* saved us and gone before us. Our life is hidden *with him* in God (Col 3:3). In faithful love he intercedes beyond all time for the life of the world. He is God's very expression of grace and truth and offers these that we may daily partake. This is possible because only Jesus is the substance of what the Mosaic law points to—the creator God who cannot brook sin and yet still loves us faithfully.

Matthew Henry writes, "From Christ we receive grace; this is a string He delights to harp upon, He cannot go off from it ... He is the true paschal lamb, the true scape-goat, the true manna."[13]

Can I receive the grace and truth that only God can give through his beloved Son?

PRAYER

Lord, thank you for grace and truth. Grant me the humility to receive these precious gifts. You are the one who speaks the truth and imparts grace into our lives of quiet desperation. Help me to share and show your grace and truth to others, that they might find peace and life with God. Amen.

* * *

---

12. Bernard, *Exegetical Commentary*, 1:30.
13. Henry, *Henry's Commentary*, 1509.

VERSES 18-23

18 No one has ever seen God;[14] the only begotten God, the One being in the embrace of the Father, He made Him known.[15]

19 And this is the testimony of John, when the Jews sent priests and Levites from Jerusalem to ask him, 'Who are you?"

20 And he confessed and did not deny, but confessed that "I am not the Christ."

21 And they asked him, "What then? Are you Elijah?" And he said, "I am not." "Are you the prophet?" And he answered, "no."

22 Therefore they said to him, "Who are you? So that we can give an answer to the ones who sent us; what do you say concerning yourself?"

23 He said,

"'I am a voice crying out in the desert,
Make straight the way of the LORD,"

As Isaiah the Prophet said.

---

14. That is, no one has ever seen God apart from the perfect revelation in the person of Jesus. What Moses experienced on Sinai was a partial manifestation of as much of the divine Person as was safe for him to experience. Recall Exod 33:17–23, especially 33:20: "'But,' He said, 'you cannot see My face, for man shall not see me and live.'" By contrast, Jesus is the very face God of God revealed to humanity, our Good Shepherd who is "gentle and humble of heart" (Matt 11:29). With him we are completely safe.

In 2 Cor 4:6 Paul writes how Jesus' light allows us to see God's glory and true nature: "... God [is] the one who said, 'out of darkness light will shine, who shone in our hearts to illuminate the knowledge of the glory of God in the face of Jesus Christ.' *Only in Jesus can we begin to know God and see His glory. By extension we can further say of John's Gospel itself that it is the exegesis or exposition to the world of God in Christ*" (Bernard, *Exegetical Commentary*, 1:33) (emph. added).

15. The root of the Greek third person aorist verb here ἐξηγήσατο gives us the English "exegesis." The word's literal sense in the Greek is to "lead out, draw out in narrative, to recount" (Robertson, *Word Pictures*, 5:18). John's witness in the prologue is that Jesus *is* the God's 'story of himself' to humanity. Only Jesus is able to "narrate God" on the plane of human existence, because only he is the Messiah to whom all the Scriptures testify ("these are they that testify concerning Me"; 5:39). The *Logos* is the Son of God bearing God's glory, showing people who God is and what he is.

John Chapter 1

✶   ✶   ✶

REFLECTION: A VOICE CALLING IN THE WILDERNESS

In response to the Jewish religious authorities who ask him "who are you?" John the Baptist paraphrases the prophet's call in Isa 40:3:

"A voice cries:
In the wilderness prepare the way of the Lord;
Make straight in the desert a highway for our God."

קוֹל קוֹרֵא
בַּמִּדְבָּר פַּנּוּ דֶּרֶךְ יְהוָה
יַשְּׁרוּ בָּעֲרָבָה מְסִלָּה לֵאלֹהֵינוּ׃

The image of the dry, barren landscape where God comes to Israel with spiritual refreshing and renewal (see ESV note) is not accidental. The desert where John the Baptist ministers mirrors Israel's spiritual condition. The Gospel's natural symbolism doesn't end there: water is most precious above all in the desert. John's ministry offering water baptism as a sign of spiritual repentance is a precursor to Jesus' offer of living water to the Samaritan woman at the well in Sychar (4:7–14), and later to the crowds in Jerusalem on the last day of the Feast of Tabernacles (7:37–39).

As Jesus' arrival does later, John the Baptist's coming disturbs the Jewish authorities, who know the ancient prophecies of a coming prophet to Israel, and fear any perceived threat to their power and control (over the Temple and Jewish religious life generally).

The prophet Malachi prophesies a coming Elijah in the Old Testament's closing verse:

> "Behold, I will send my messenger, and he will prepare the way before me...
> I will send you Elijah the prophet before the great and awesome day of the Lord comes.
> And he will turn the hearts of the fathers to their children and the hearts of children to their fathers, lest I come and strike the land with a decree of utter destruction." (Mal 3:1, 4:5–6)

Moses also promises Israel the future raising up by God of "a prophet like me" in Deut 18:15.

Interestingly, John the Baptist in 1:21 disclaims any link with the *historical* Elijah, saying in effect that he is not the 8th century BC prophet Elijah in person who prophesied against Ahab, one of Israel's wicked kings. (According 2 Kgs 2:11, this Elijah did not actually die, but "went up by a whirlwind to heaven"). At the same time, Jesus affirms John the Baptist as fulfilling the prophecy about *a future* Elijah in Matthew 11:14, where He says, "For all the Prophets and the Law prophesied until John [that is, John the Baptist], and if you are willing to accept it, he is Elijah *who is to come*" (emph. added).

In 1:21 John the Baptist also denies that he is "the Prophet" for Israel promised by Moses in Deut 18:15 – because the Prophet is Jesus, as John (the disciple) records later in his gospel after Christ's feeding of the five thousand in John 6:14:

> "When the people saw the sign that He had done, they said, 'This is indeed the Prophet, who is to come into the world.'"

Matthew Henry notes that the Deuteronomy reference "is primarily intended as a promise of Christ, and it is the clearest promise of Him in all the law of Moses"[16].

Through this testimony, John the Baptist "makes way" for the one who fulfills this and every other Messianic prophecy recorded in the Hebrew scriptures.

PRAYER

Father, of the many voices we hear at Christmas and other times of the year, most have far to do more with advertising, entertainment, and other pretexts for personal gratification than with Jesus.

John the Baptist had his priorities right. Help me to hear his call to repentance, and to reflect on what the coming of the kingdom of heaven calls me to do in this season of my life. In your name, Amen.

* * *

VERSES 24–38

24 And they were sent from the Pharisees.
25 And they asked Him and said to Him, "Why therefore are you baptizing if you are neither the Christ nor Elijah nor the Prophet?"[17]

---

16. Henry, *Henry's Commentary*, 190.

17. John's baptizing activity, and who he was baptizing, is the reason these representatives of the Pharisees approach him. "The baptism of proselytes . . . was a recognized, if not a universal, practice in [Judaism] at this time. But why should *Jews* be baptized? And what authority had John to exercise this ministry? Baptism . . . a symbolic rite of purification, would indeed be a token of the approach of the Messianic kingdom" (Bernard, *Exegetical Commentary*, 1:30, *citing* Ezekiel 36:25: "I will sprinkle clean water on you,

26 John answered them saying, "I baptize in water; there stands among you One whom you do not know,

27 The One coming after me, whose sandal strap I am not worthy to untie."[18]

28 These things took place at Bethany beyond the Jordan, where John was baptizing.

29 On the next day he saw Jesus coming to him and said, "Behold the Lamb of God, the one who takes away the sin of the world."[19]

30 It is He of whom I said, "After me comes a man who takes precedence over me, because He was before me.

---

and you shall be clean from all your uncleannesses, and from all your idols I will cleanse you"; also Zech 13:1 and its mention of a fountain to be opened for the house of David and inhabitants of Jerusalem, "to cleanse them from sin and uncleanness"). The issue was that John with his admission in 1:21 had already disclaimed all of the known 'standing' according to Jewish tradition to be ministering such a baptism.

This context helps us better understand why the Pharisees' representatives are challenging John the Baptist's authority to baptize Jewish believers in preparation for the 'new kingdom' he says he is announcing—in short, he doesn't fit the expected paradigm. In the Pharisees' eyes, given his admission in 1:21 he is neither the Messiah, Elijah, nor "the prophet," i.e., one of the end-time figures recognized in Jewish tradition, John the Baptist is—like Jesus the very Messiah he heralds—highly unorthodox and therefore suspect. See Carson, *According to John*, 145.

We can see also the contrast here between John the Baptist's water baptism of repentance and the baptism by the Holy Spirit that only a few verses later (see 1:33) John testifies that Jesus will perform as Messiah.

18. In first-century Israel, the duty of unfastening a master's shoes was counted as a household slave's duty (Bernard, *Exegetical Commentary*, 1:41).

19. Recall Isa 53:6, 7:

"All we like sheep have gone astray; we have turned – every one – to his own way.
And the LORD has laid on Him the iniquity of us all . . .
He was oppressed, and He was afflicted, yet He opened not His mouth;
like a lamb that is led to the slaughter . . . "

Even though the idea of a suffering Messiah may not have been prevalent among the first-century Jewish community, John the Baptist's prophetic enunciation as he meets Jesus for the first time identifies him in precisely this way. John understands that Jesus is the true Paschal Lamb of whom all earlier Passover sacrifices had been but a type (Bernard, *Exegetical Commentary*, 1:44–45).

Why does Jesus say of John the Baptist, "among those born of women there has arisen no one greater than [John]" (Matt 11:11)? Because John identifies Jesus precisely as the eternal Paschal Lamb offered up as blessed provision for us. Paul voices the same truth in 1 Cor 5:7b-8: "For Christ our Passover Lamb has been sacrificed. Let us therefore keep the feast . . ."

31 And I did not know Him, but so that He might be revealed to Israel, for this reason I came baptizing with water."[20]

32 And John bore witness, saying that "I saw the Spirit coming down as a dove out of heaven and it remained upon Him.

33 And I did not know Him, but the One who sent me to baptize with water, He said to me, 'the One upon whom you may the Spirit coming down and remaining upon Him, He is the One baptizing with the Holy Spirit.'

34 And I have seen and I have testified that He is the Son of God."[21]

35 The next day again John was standing with two of his disciples

36 and looking at Jesus as he walked by he said, "Behold, the Lamb of God!"[22]

37 And the two disciples heard him speaking and followed Jesus.

38 And Jesus turned and seeing them following said to them, "What are you looking for?"

And they answered Him, "Rabbi," which translated means 'Teacher,' "where are you staying?"

* * *

REFLECTION: WHAT ARE YOU LOOKING FOR?

In his 1926 poem "Once by the Pacific," Robert Frost recalls a time from his early childhood when he was briefly alone while walking with his parents on San Francisco's Ocean Beach during a gathering storm:

---

20. John the Baptist is saying that until he saw the dove alighting upon Jesus (recounted in each of the Synoptic gospels, Matt 3:16, Mark 1:10 and Luke 3:22) as the sign from God (1:32–34), he did not know Jesus was the Messiah.

21. This is the title given to Jesus by God at his baptism: "This is My Son, the Beloved, with whom I am well pleased" (Matt 3:17; see also Luke 3:22). "The Son as the recipient of the Spirit is the one the Father loves. As *Son of God*, Jesus brings delight to the heart of the Father, and also to our hearts as we follow him" (Milne, *Message of John*, 55). As prophesied by Isaiah, Jesus as God's Son is Messiah, the chosen servant whom God anoints with the Holy Spirit and who brings justice to the earth:

> "Behold My servant, whom I uphold,
> My chosen, in whom my soul delights,
> I have put my Spirit upon Him;
> He will bring forth justice to the nations" (Isa 42:1).

22. Reflecting John (the Apostle's) fondness for the number seven, in this encounter with John the Baptist and (soon after) with several of the men who would become Jesus' own disciples, Christ is called by seven titles: Lamb of God (1:36), Rabbi (1:38), Messiah (1:41), Jesus of Nazareth (1:45), Son of God (1:49), King of Israel (1:49) and Son of Man (1:51). See discussion at BibleProject, "John 1–12."

> "The shattered water made a misty din.
> Great waves looked over others coming in,
> And thought of doing something to the shore
> That water never did to land before...
> It looked as if a night of dark intent
> Was coming, and not only a night, an age.
> Someone had better be prepared for rage.
> There would be more than ocean-water broken
> Before God's last 'Put out the light' was spoken."

God may not have yet put out the last light, but it's hard to deny that our world seems increasingly dark and weary.

Dystopian themes dominate the news—war, disease, food scarcity, and the grim harvest of a fully intentional progressive/woke assault on traditional values occupy national and world headlines. Russia, Ukraine, China, and Taiwan. Escalating hostility and violence against Jews and Christians. At the same time, 'under the headlines' millions of the world's poor (predominantly women and children) face an epidemic of violence and human trafficking, slavery, and sexual exploitation. Even Mother Earth and our climate seem to be literally wearing out with time, bearing the burden of human exploitation and excess.

The daily headlines serve us up a lot to hold, too much it feels like. Against such a backdrop, what are you seeking in your life, in this age?

One thing I seek is a better understanding of the meaning behind—perhaps "above" is a better word—suffering. In his May 2021 *Atlantic* article "Growing My Faith in the Face of Death," Tim Keller trenchantly observes that we in the US (and the West generally) seek to avoid pain at all costs, and are (i) both far less equipped than to deal with suffering than those in more ancient but currently less 'fortunate,' less 'comfortable' cultures in the developing world (the Global South, including South Asia and Africa, and the Middle East in particular), and (ii) far more traumatized by it.

Certainly, I'm no exception. The first two times I went through chemotherapy, I played a mind game with myself, treating it like an extended workout I had only to persevere in order to get through. I prayed often, but when suffering came, as it did at times during those treatments, and in a much more toxic and continuous form during the most recent round of treatment, the truth is I just wanted to escape. The mental anguish of undergoing the side effects was as traumatic as their actual physical symptoms.

Cancer has sharpened my awareness of how fleeting time is and how precious is life. And of the basic fact that, contrary to everything our age of technology would otherwise have us believe, I am not in control. Before my diagnosis, I lived and imagined otherwise, but I do not control the number of my days on the earth, and I am most assuredly not the "captain of my soul."

God's "answer" to the reality of suffering, so far as I've been able to discern it, is often to redirect our perspective: he tells us not to fear and asks our trust and reliance on him. Even when we face circumstances seemingly beyond our capacity to endure, in our own or others' suffering. Even when he appears silent, as he was when Jesus cried out the opening words of Ps 22 on the cross:

> "And about the ninth hour Jesus cried out with a loud voice, saying, ⸢ηλι ηλι⸣ ⸢λεμα σαβαχθανι⸣;
> that is, "My God, my God, why have you forsaken me?" (Matt 27:45)

Am I willing to accept that and trust in Him, no matter what? Jesus did, and won the ultimate victory:

> ". . . who, though He was in the form of God, did not count equality with God something to be grasped,
> But made Himself nothing, taking the form of a servant . . .
> And being found in human formed, He humbled Himself be becoming obedient to the point of death, even death on a cross.
> Therefore God has highly exalted Him and bestowed on Him the name that is above every name . . ." (Phil 2:6–9).

> "Blessed be the...God of all comfort, who comforts us in all our affliction, so that we may be able to comfort those who are in any affliction, with the comfort with which we ourselves are comforted by God" (1 Cor 1:3–4).

As the Easter saying goes, it may be Friday, but praise God, Sunday's comin'!

PRAYER

Lord Jesus, I look and I seek many things, but without you I am lost. Illuminate the darkness in my life with your light, your life. Walk with me through the valley of death, and all the way home to glory in your house in the new heaven and the new earth. Amen.

* * *

VERSES 39-51

39 He said to them, "Come and you will see."[23]

---

23. Jesus always welcomes those who seek and ask.

John Chapter 1

Then they came and saw where He was staying and stayed with Him that day; it was about the tenth hour.[24]

40 Andrew, the brother of Simon Peter, was one of the two disciples who heard John and followed Him;

41 He first found[25] his own brother Simon and said to him, "We have found the Messiah" (which is translated Christ);

42 He led him to Jesus. Looking at him Jesus said, "You are Simon, son of John; you will be called Kephas,"[26] which means rock."

43 The next day He decided to go to Galilee, and He found Philip. And Jesus said to him, "Follow me."

44 Philip was from Bethsaida, the city of Andrew and Peter.

45 Philip found Nathaniel[27] and said to him, "We have found the One of whom Moses in the Law and also the Prophets wrote,[28] Jesus son of Joseph of Nazareth."[29]

46 And Nathaniel said to him, "Can anything good come out of Nazareth?"[30] And Philip said to him, "Come and see."[31]

47 Jesus saw Nathaniel coming to Him and said of him, "Behold, a true Israelite in whom there is no deceit!"[32]

48 Nathaniel said to Him, "How do you know me?"

---

24. In the Jewish system that counts hours of the day from sunrise, this would have been approximately 4 PM.

25. Peter was the first convert led to Christ by a disciple (Metzger, *Textual Commentary*, 172).

26. *Kephas* is Aramaic for "rock." "When Jesus later prays for Peter that his faith might not fail, then He *made him* what He here called him—a stone" (Henry, *Henry's Commentary*, 1512).

27. Nathaniel is a Hebrew name, meaning "God has given," the equivalent of the Greek Theodore (Bernard, *Exegetical Commentary*, 1:61).

28. Reflecting John's basic stance throughout his gospel, namely that Jesus fulfills the Old Testament scriptures (Carson, *According to John*, 159).

29. Interestingly, John simply records without further comment Philip's mistaken understanding of Jesus' parentage, trusting that his readers are of one mind with him (John) that Jesus is "the only-begotten God, the One in the bosom of the Father" (1:18) (Bernard, *Exegetical Commentary*, 1:62).

30. Since Nazareth is not mentioned in the Old Testament, there was nothing in Jewish tradition to connect this city with Messianic prophecy (Bernard, *Exegetical Commentary*, 1:62).

31. Echoing Jesus' own invitation 1:3 to Andrew and one other unnamed disciple (most likely John himself) (ESV note).

32. Jesus immediately recognizes the true nature of each person that he meets.

Jesus answered and said to him, "Before Philip called you, I saw you under the fig tree."

49 Nathaniel answered Him, "Rabbi, You are the Son of God; you are the King of Israel."[33]

50 Jesus answered and said to him, "Because I said to you that I saw you under the fig tree, you believe? You will see greater things than these."

51 And He said to him, "Truly, truly I say to you all, you all will see the heavens opening and the angels of God ascending and descending on the Son of Man."

* * *

REFLECTION: JACOB'S LADDER AND THE SON OF MAN

Nathaniel is direct to the point of abruptness in 1:48 when he asks Jesus, "how do You know me?"

Jesus answers just as directly, citing Jacob's dream at Bethel of the heavenly ladder recorded in Gen 28:12 to confirm his identity of the Messianic Son of God, "the meeting point between heaven's fullness and earth's need[34]":

> "Jacob left Beersheba and went toward Haran.
> And he came to a certain place and stayed there that night, because the sun had set...
> And he dreamed, and behold, there was a ladder set upon the earth, and the top of it reached to heaven.
> And behold, the angels of God were ascending and descending on it!"

In his paraphrase of Jacob's vision, however, Jesus substitutes himself, bearing the title "Son of Man," for Jacob's ladder.

What's going on here? In first century Israel, the designation 'Son of Man' was not a known title for the Messiah. Jesus thus was able "to take up the expression and fill it with what significance He chose." The clear Old Testament

---

33. Echoing John the Baptist, Nathaniel the 'true Israelite' in effect acclaims Jesus as the Messiah. "Son of God" and "King of Israel" are both Messianic titles having their roots in Psalm 2 (Bruce, *Gospel of John*, 61; Bernard, *Exegetical Commentary*, 1:64):

> ". . . I have set my king on Zion, my holy hill . . .
> You are my Son; today I have begotten you.
> Ask of me, and I will make the nations your heritage, and the ends of the earth Your possession . . .
> Kiss the Son, lest He be angry and you perish in the way,
> For His wrath is quickly kindled.
> Blessed are all who take refuge in Him" (Ps 2:6–8, 12).

34. Milne, *Message of John*, 61.

reference generally to "son of man" comes in Daniel's vision of the day of judgment, where the one coming with the clouds of heaven "like a son of man" (כְּבַר אֱנָשׁ in the Aramaic; that is, a human figure) is given universal authority and an everlasting kingdom (Dan 7:13, 14)[35].

Jesus' point with this substitution is that He *is* the ladder that Jacob dreamt of, the only way to the Father in heaven (John 14:6).

Like all faithful Jews, the disciples would have honored Jacob as the father of the twelve tribes, and Beth-El itself as the locus of his vision of heaven and where he heard God's promises about the land, the Hebrew nation, and God's presence with them to accomplish his promises. But Jesus here goes further, declaring that *wherever* he abides is a new 'Beth-El,' or House of God. Can this be said of our hearts, our bodies (Eph 3:17; 1 Cor 6:19)?

Like Nathaniel, you could ask Jesus, 'how do you know me?' As you reflect on his answer, consider honestly your relationship with him and his calling for you today. Then pray for the grace and courage to pursue that calling.

* * *

---

35. Bruce, *Gospel of John*, 63.

2

John Chapter 2

VERSES 1-12

1 On the third day a wedding took place in Cana in Galilee, and the mother of Jesus was there.
2 And Jesus was also invited to the wedding along with His disciples.[1]
3 And when the wine ran out, Jesus' mother said to Him, "They have no wine."
4 Jesus said to her, "What is that to me and to you, woman? My hour has not yet come."[2]
5 His mother said to the servants, "Whatever He says to you, do it."

---

1. Cana is the first of a series of episodes (spanning 2:13–12:50) that John records involving Jesus' encounters with a specific element of Jewish culture and faith (a wedding, Rabbinic authority, water and a sacred well, and the temple). In each of the stories, the miraculous sign that Christ performs reveals that he is in fact the embodied fulfillment of each institution and also forces people to decide what they think about Him. See BibleProject, "BibleProject."

These stories can similarly be read as John locating his narrative within a series of Jewish festivals, where in each case "Jesus fulfills some aspect of messianic expectations associated with that feast" (Fee and Stuart, *How to Read the Bible*, 309).

2. Jesus' reply to his mother reflects a keen awareness of his appointed hour—the time of his appearance as the true 'King of Israel' (as Nathaniel declared in 1:49) who would fulfill the Abrahamic covenant ("in you all the families of the earth will be blessed" (Gen 12:3) by redeeming, through his death, everyone throughout history willing to receive him as Savior.

John Chapter 2

6 And there were six stone water jars there for the Jewish purification rites, holding twenty or thirty gallons each.

7 Jesus said to them, "Fill the jars with water." And they filled them to the brim.

8 And He said to them, "Now draw some out and take [it] to the master of the feast." And they took [it].

9 When the master of the feast tasted the water that had become wine and did not know where it came from (but the servants knew having drawn the water), he called the bridegroom

10 And said to him, "Everyone first serves the good wine and when the guests have drunk freely, the inferior wine; you have kept the good wine until now."

11 This the first of His signs Jesus did in Cana of Galilee, and revealed His glory, and His disciples believed in Him.

12 After this He went down to Capernaum [*Kapharnaom*] with His mother and His brothers and His disciples, and they stayed there for a few days.

* * *

REFLECTION: SIGNS

John's gospel has been called the Book of Signs. John writes that the miracle of the water becoming wine at the wedding in Cana is the first of Jesus' "signs" (2:11).

In the Hebrew scriptures, the phrase "signs and wonders" is often used to describe the wondrous power of God's supernatural activity, for example in Exod 7:3 where God tells Moses His plan for Egypt:

וַאֲנִי אַקְשֶׁה אֶת־לֵב פַּרְעֹה
וְהִרְבֵּיתִי אֶת־אֹתֹתַי וְאֶת־מוֹפְתַי בְּאֶרֶץ מִצְרָיִם:

"But I will harden Pharaoh's heart, that I may multiply my signs and wonders in the land of Egypt."

But what does John mean by "signs"? Most simply, the term in the Greek (σημείων) means "miracles." But the miracles John records Jesus performing during His earthly ministry are never simply naked displays of supernatural power. Rather, each miracle points beyond itself to an underlying reality—namely, God himself and the coming of his kingdom and fulfilment of Old Testament Messianic prophecy in the person of Christ.[3]

---

3. Carson, *According to John*, 175; Bruce, *Gospel of John*, 72.

How many "signs" did Jesus perform? John records seven, the biblical number of perfection (some commentators treat his feeding the five thousand and walking on water in chapter 6 as a single sign, and the seventh sign as Jesus' own resurrection):

- changing the water to wine at the Cana wedding (2:1–11),
- healing the royal official's son (4:46–54),
- healing the paralytic at the Bethesda pool in Jerusalem (5:1–18),
- feeding the five thousand with five barley loaves and two fish (6:1–14),
- walking on the water (6:16–26), and
- raising Lazarus from the dead (11:1–47).

Are these the only miracles Jesus performed? John makes clear that he has recorded only some of the miracles Jesus did, but he does so for a specific purpose:

> Now Jesus did many other signs in the presence of the disciples, which are not written in this book, *but these are written so that you may believe that Jesus is the Christ, and that by believing you have life in His name* (21:30–31) (emph. added).

In this first of his recorded "signs," Jesus blesses the wedding by bringing forth excellent new wine from water. The wedding feast foreshadows the feast at Christ's parousia (his second coming) at which he will inaugurate the new heaven and the new earth (Rev 21:1–7). Which is to say that Jesus Messiah is the "better wine" which God has saved until "just the right time" (Gal 4:4) to redeem people out from under the curse of sin and judgment under the law. In this way, Christ fulfills the prophecy in Isaiah 26 of the great messianic feast of nations welcomed by God, at which the wine is *very good*:

> "On this mountain the Lord of hosts will make for all peoples
> a feast of rich food, a feast of well-aged wine.
> and He will swallow up on this mountain the covering that is cast over all peoples,
> the veil that is spread over all nations.
> He will swallow up death forever, and the Lord God will wipe away tears from all faces"
> (Isa 25:6–8; John sees the vision of Isaiah's prophecy fulfilled in Rev 19:6–9).

As you reflect on the wedding at Cana, consider the following:

- The "large quantity and high quality" (ESV study note, 2:11) of the wine that Jesus produces at the host's moment of greatest need. The abundant, excellent wine and its miraculous appearance point to 1) Jesus'

own messianic character and identity, 2) the abundant blessing possible in His presence and 3) God's overflowing generosity to us in Christ.
- The connection between the abundant wine at Cana and even more miraculous "new covenant in My blood" (1 Cor 11:25) given by Jesus for his flock at the Last Supper.
- Soon after Cana, John identifies the destroyed and resurrected temple with Jesus' own body (2:20–21). Cana and the other "signs" in Jesus' ministry that John records all "point to and find their fulfillment in [Jesus'] death and resurrection." Cana introduces a theme that John continues in the following stories of Nicodemus, the testimony of John the Baptist, the Samaritan woman at the well and the healing of the Gentile official's son (2:23–4:54), which is that "Jesus brings a new age which the old order of [the Mosaic law] was unable to achieve"[4].
- Lastly, the fact that since Jesus' hour as Messiah has come, we are living in days of grace until He comes again.

What new wine might Jesus give to you and through you, to others, if you offer to him your jars of mere water and let him do his work?

* * *

VERSES 13-25

13 The *Pascha* [Passover] of the Jews was at hand, and Jesus went up to Jerusalem.[5]

---

4. Ellis, *World of St. John*, 62–63.

5. The Jewish high holidays figure prominently throughout John's narrative.
We find in fact seven feasts mentioned in the gospel (Arnette, "Seven Feasts in John's Gospel"):
- Passover, appearing three times (2:13, 6:4, 11:55);
- An unnamed feast in 5:1 (possibly the Feast of Trumpets (what we know today as *Rosh Hashana*, or New Year's Day in the Jewish calendar) marking the beginning of a new agricultural year and cycle, Lev 23:23–25; see Bruce, *Gospel of John*, 121);
- Tabernacles, or the Feast of Booths (7:2);
- "the great day" of Tabernacles in 7:37; and
- the Feast of Dedication (celebrating rededication of the Temple in December 164 B.C., after its desecration by Seleucid rule Antiochus Epiphanes IV in 167 (ESV Study Note)).

The first Passover John mentions, in chapter 2, and the Jerusalem Temple provide the

14 And He found in the Temple people selling oxen and sheep and doves, and moneychangers also sitting there,

15 And making a whip out of cords he drove them all out of the Temple, with the sheep and the oxen, and poured out the coins and overturned the tables of the moneychangers,

16 And to the people selling pigeons He said, "Take these things away; do not make My Father's house a marketplace!"

17 His disciples remembered that it is written,
'The zeal of Your house will consume me.'[6]

18 The Jews answered and said to Him, "What sign do you show us that you are doing these things?"[7]

19 Jesus answered and said to them, "Destroy this temple and in three days I will raise it up."

20 Then the Jews said, "This temple was built in forty-six years, and you will raise it in three days?"

21 But He was speaking concerning the Temple of His body.[8]

---

perfect setting for Christ's emphasis on holiness and proper worship as he cleanses the temple from the commercial practices permitted by the high priest and other temple authorities:

> "John . . . uses the meaning of [the annual Jewish] feasts to throw into relief the claims Jesus makes and the fulfilment he brings to the promise inherent in Judaism . . . The Passover festival, deriving from the exodus from Egypt (*cf.* Exod chapters 12–13), was celebrated primarily in the temple, the perceived 'seat' of the living God, and hence the source of the holiness both of the city [Jerusalem] and the nation [of Israel]. The cleansing of the temple which Jesus effects during the feast is an impressive statement both of his personal authority and of the crisis which his mission represented for Judaism" (Milne, *Message of John*, 67).

6. Knowing its intended purpose as God's "house of prayer" (Isa 56:7), Jesus' zeal for the sanctity of the temple prompts the disciples to remember the Messianic prophecy of Ps 69:9 that "zeal for your house has consumed me."

Psalm 69 is widely cited in the New Testament, both elsewhere in John (15:25; citing Psalm 69:4), Acts 1:20 (citing Psalm 69:25), Romans 15:3 (citing Psalm 69:9), and Romans 11:9–10 (citing Psalm 69:22–23) (Bernard, *Exegetical Commentary*, 1:92).

"Jesus' cleansing of the temple testifies to His concern for pure worship, a right relationship with God at the place supremely designated to serve as the focal point of the relationship between God and man" (Carson, *According to John*, 180). Jesus 'consuming zeal' is also precisely what attracts opposition from the religious establishment and leads ultimately to his death on the cross.

7. The Jewish leaders in the synagogue demand a sign as proof for the authority Jesus asserts over the temple, mistakenly surmising that he can't satisfy their request (Bernard, *Exegetical Commentary*, 1:92). Jesus answers immediately, with an ironic prophecy of his own resurrection (as John attests in v.21).

8. Jesus in effect claims preeminence over the temple itself, based on the fact that his

22 Therefore when He was raised from the dead, His disciples remembered that He said this and believed the Scripture[9] and the word Jesus that spoke.

23 And when He was in Jerusalem at the Feast of Passover, many believed in His name when they saw the signs that He was doing.

24 But Jesus for His part did not entrust Himself to them, because He knew all people

25 And because He had no need for anyone to bear witness concerning man; for He knew what was in man.

* * *

REFLECTION: WHAT'S IN MAN

Jesus was fooled by no one. He indeed "knew what was in man." Jesus knew then, and He knows now.
That is a most unsettling thought. It means that all of my pretense falls away before the Lord. He knows what's in me, all of it, and has the measure of me. Against that sobering prospect however is the miracle that knowing all of that, and setting aside also any illusion of 'moral standing,' Jesus somehow still loves us unconditionally.

PRAYER

Lord, may I love others today with something approximating the measure of grace which you first loved me. Jesus knows what lies within, and still he loves me, even me! Praise God, Amen.

* * *

---

actual body is "living habitation of God on earth" (Bruce, *Gospel of John*, 77).

9. By "Scripture" (literally, "writing"), some commentators (NICNT) believe that John's reference to "the Scripture" here is the text from Psalm 69:9, which is quoted directly in v.19, while others (Carson, *According to John*, 183) identify Ps 16:10 as the possible reference: "For You will not abandon my soul to Sheol, or let Your holy one see corruption."

3

John Chapter 3

VERSES 1-21

1 There was a man of the Pharisees named Nicodemus, a leader of the Jews;
2 He went to Him[1] by night and said to Him, "Rabbi, we know that You have come as a teacher from God; for no one is able to do these signs that You are doing, unless God is with him."
3 Jesus answered and said to him, "Truly, truly I say to you, unless one is born again, he cannot see the Kingdom of God."[2]

---

1. That is, Jesus.

2. Nicodemus appears in John's Gospel as a figure of rabbinic authority. His seemingly polite greeting initially masks an attempt, like others who questioned Jesus' asserted identity and role, to establish the criteria by which to judge who Jesus is. Jesus however sees through the subterfuge immediately and rejects Nicodemus's premise by challenging his standing to discern heavenly matters in this first place.

When Jesus mentions "to see the kingdom of God," he means to recognize the saving reign of God. For a Jew of Nicodemus's background and beliefs, to "see the Kingdom of God" would have meant to participate in the kingdom at the end of the age, and to experience eternal, resurrection life (Carson, *According to John*, 188).

Perhaps not surprisingly, Nicodemus claims that he can recognize Jesus is from God based on the miracles this "Rabbi" has done. Jesus, however, insists that it is not a matter of new teaching that Israel needs, but rather a new heart and new life, a radically different kind of life: only one who is born again can truly "see" and understand God's love and salvation offered to humanity, including but not limited to miraculous signs done by God's power. In doing so, Jesus lays bare Nicodemus's own need for God's salvation. Nicodemus comes by night under a pretense of theological skepticism; Christ answers with a revelation of Nicodemus's (and by extension the Israelite nation's) spiritual desolation

4 Nicodemus said to Him, "How can anyone who is old be born again? Is it not impossible for a person to enter his mother's womb a second time and be born?"
5 Jesus answered, "Truly, truly I say to you, unless someone is born of water and the Spirit,[3] it is not possible to enter the kingdom of God.
6 The one born of the flesh is flesh and the one born of the Spirit is spirit.
7 Do not marvel that I said to you 'you[4] must be born again.'
8 The wind blows where it wishes, and you hear its sound, but you do not know from whence it comes and where it goes. So it is with everyone born of the Spirit."[5]
9 Nicodemus answered and said to Him, "How are these things possible?"
10 Jesus answered and said to him, "You are Israel's teacher and you do not know these things?

---

which only the Messiah-now-come can heal.

3. Rebutting Nicodemus' incredulity, Jesus paraphrases Ezekiel 36:25–27 to emphasize the necessity of spiritual rebirth for salvation:

> "*I* will sprinkle clean water on you, and you shall be clean from all your uncleannesses, and from all your idols *I* will cleanse you.
> And *I* will give you a new heart, and a new spirit *I* will put within you. And *I* will remove the heart of stone from your flesh and give you a heart of flesh.
> And *I* will put my Spirit within you, and cause you to walk in my statutes and be careful to obey my rules" (ESV; emph. added).

With six references to "I" in the first-person verb forms of the Hebrew as the "Lord God" speaks in this passage, Ezekiel emphasizes that it is *God* who initiates the action of spiritual renewal by cleansing and preparing the heart of a person to "see" and understand the truth of God's love and his/her need for it. Salvation is not a matter of human initiative or reformation but instead quite simply a gift of God. The remainder of Jesus' exchange with Nicodemus testifies that the form of the gift is in fact Christ himself.

4. Interestingly, in the Greek, the first "you" here is singular, while the second is plural (meaning "you all," or in other words "even you Pharisees"!). In v.12, both times "you" is used the form is plural, as Jesus calls out not only to Nicodemus's but the Pharisees' unbelief.

5. The key point about the wind is "its essential mysteriousness. While today we have better knowledge of its origin and nature, we have no better mastery of its direction [than in antiquity]. Essentially therefore, the new birth is from God; it is supernatural, beyond human control or exhaustive human knowledge. Like the wind, however, and despite its mysteriousness, its effects can be experienced at first hand" (Milne, *Message of John*, 76).

In other words, the Holy Spirit works solely according to the will of God, not the expectation of man. The occasion of God's salvation or blessing can arise at both unexpected as well as hoped-for times and occasions.

11 Truly, truly I say to you that We speak that which We know and We bear witness to that which We have seen, and you do not receive Our testimony.[6]
12 If I spoke to you of earthly things and you do not believe, how will you believe if I tell you of heavenly things?
13 And no one has gone up into heaven except the one who came down from heaven, the Son of Man.
14 And just as Moses lifted upon the serpent in the desert, so the Son of Man must be lifted up,
15 So that everyone believing in Him might have eternal life.[7]

16 For God so loved the world that He gave His Only Begotten Son, so that whoever believes in Him may not perish, but have eternal life.

17 For God did not send the Son into the world in order to judge the world, but in order that the world might be saved through Him.[8]

---

6. Again, the Greek form of the verb here "you do not receive" is plural, as Jesus continues his spiritual diagnosis of the Pharisee leaders including Nicodemus himself.

7. Jesus' reference here to Moses lifting up the bronze serpent on a pole in Num 21:4–9 prefigures His own 'lifting up' on the Cross at Golgotha, opening the way God's salvation for the people of the earth (Bernard, *Critical and Exegetical Commentary*, 1:115). In doing so, Christ is teaching Nicodemus "Israel's teacher" that "the new day of cleansing and power anticipated by Ezekiel (in the passage referenced in verses 5–8 above) is now at hand, *that the long-awaited messianic age is now present*. This is because the King, the Messiah—Jesus himself—is now present. For entry to this kingdom, racial inheritance, circumcision, energetic law-keeping, acts of piety or scriptural knowledge, avail nothing. What is needed is the receiving of a new spiritual life from God (*cf.* 1:12–14) through personal faith in Jesus himself as the one who had come from God (3:14f.), and was to be *lifted up* as the object of faith" (Milne, *Message of John*, 76).

8. Both the object of God's love and scope of Jesus' salvific power is "the world" (κόσμος). In the Greek, κόσμος means both "the sum total of everything here and now, the world" and "all humanity" (BDAG, 561–63). The term was used by both Plato and Aristotle to mean "the universe," and according to Platonist philosopher Plutarch, the sixth-century BC Greek philosopher Pythagoras was the first to use the word this way, in the context of describing the order of the material world. The idea of a totality of the natural world is "thoroughly Greek and without early Hebrew counterpart." In the New Testament, the word is used to refer to the material universe as distinct from God (see for example John 21:25), but including "the world of moral agents as well as the sum of physical forces. That is, it stands for mankind at large, as well as for the earth" (Bernard, *Exegetical Commentary*, 1:12).

John Chapter 3

18 The one believing in Him is not judged; but the one not believing has already been judged, because he has not believed in the Name of the Only Begotten Son of God.[9]

19 And this is the judgment, that the light has come into the world and people loved the darkness more than the light; for their deeds were evil.

20 For everyone doing evil hates the light and does not come to the light, lest his deeds be exposed;[10]

21 But the one doing the truth comes to the light, so that it might be revealed that his works are done in God."

* * *

A MORNING PRAYER

Lord, each day that you give us to live in this beautiful, broken world in your infinite mercy, may we walk in the light of your truth to us in Christ, that our works might be revealed as having been done in you. Give us the heart, mind, and commitment to do your will.

In your blessed name, Amen.

* * *

VERSES 22–30

22 After these things Jesus and His disciples went into the land of Judah and He stayed there with them and was baptizing.[11]

23 And John also was baptizing at Aenon near Salim, because there was much water there, and they were coming and being baptized.

24 For John had not yet been thrown into prison.

---

9. In the Jewish eschatology of John's time, the Messiah was to come as the judge of humanity. John takes pains to emphasize in these verses that Jesus' mission in the mind of God is to ensure that *everyone* who believes in Christ has eternal life (Bernard, *Exegetical Commentary*, 1:119).

10. Jesus here highlights "the working out of a moral law. The root of unbelief in Christ is the refusal to turn to His light, because man's conduct will not bear scrutiny" (Bernard, *Exegetical Commentary*, 1:121).

11. Taking account of 4:2's statement "(although Jesus himself did not baptize, but only his disciples)," commentators have consistently interpreted John's phrase "and was baptizing" in 3:22 to mean that Jesus was supervising his disciples who were baptizing in his name (Bernard, *Exegetical Commentary*, 1:127–28; Henry, *Henry's Commentary*, 1522; ESV study note).

25 There then arose a debate between John's disciples and the Jews concerning baptism.

26 And they [John's disciples] went to John and said to him, "Rabbi, He who was with you across the Jordan, the one to Whom you have witnessed; behold, He is baptizing and everyone is going to Him."[12]

27 John answered and said, "A man cannot receive anything except what has been given to him from heaven.[13]

28 You yourselves are witnesses for me that I said, I am not the Christ, but that I am sent before Him.

29 The one having the bride, he is the bridegroom; the friend of the bridegroom is the one standing and hearing him rejoices greatly at the voice of the bridegroom. Therefore this joy of mine has been fulfilled.

30 It is necessary for Him to increase, and for me to become less."

* * *

REFLECTION: DON'T BE OFFENDED

"It is necessary for Him to increase, for me to become less" (John 3:30).

With these words, John the Baptist completes his testimony about Jesus the Messiah. Matthew 11:11 records Jesus' testimony about John this way: "among those born of women there has arisen no one greater than John the Baptist. Yet the one who is least in the kingdom of heaven is greater than he."

John the Baptist saw the full import of Jesus' coming as the New Elijah, the Lamb of God. He told the whole truth and nothing but the truth about Jesus. John came, baptizing and witnessing, that Jesus "might be revealed to Israel" (John 1:31). Jesus' own witness about John in Matthew's Gospel leaves no doubt about the greatness of John's prophetic ministry and message.

But John also paid the price for his witness about Jesus, dying in all likelihood alone in a Herodian prison, beheaded at the urging of the daughter of Herodias, Herod's brother Philip's wife.

---

12. Note John's disciples' competitive ministry concerns. They are jealous and angry that another teacher should be invading what they have counted as their master's prerogative (Bernard, *Exegetical Commentary*, 1:130). Jesus' disciples weren't the only ones who were prone to think in human political terms rather those of the kingdom!

13. John here reminds his disciples of a great principle of life, namely that all the gifts we have are only from heaven. "Different employments are according to the direction of divine Providence, different endowments according to the distribution of the divine grace. We should not envy those that have a larger share of gifts than we have, or that move in a larger sphere of usefulness" (Henry, *Henry's Commentary*, 1521).

The end of John's life on earth raises a question: If John was as great as Jesus said he was, why didn't Jesus use his power to save him from Herod's prison and death by beheading?

Scripture doesn't say. We also don't know how John may have felt during his last days in prison. Did he ever feel forgotten and forsaken? We do know that before he was murdered, after hearing of Jesus' miraculous deeds, John sent disciples to ask Jesus "Are you the one who is to come, or shall we look for another?" (Matt 11:2).

Jesus in response lists the healing, resurrections and teaching that he has done, and then concludes with the mysterious statement "And blessed is the one who is not offended by Me" (Matt 2:6). Jesus in effect lets his deeds speak for themselves and then abruptly warns John not to be offended. Jesus basically says, "'Be careful, John, that after coming this far, you don't fail, you don't turn away because of offense.' And shortly after this, John is executed. God appears very willing to offend."[14]

In the trial (whether from setbacks from cancer or otherwise), will I be offended, or keep looking to Jesus?

PRAYER

Lord, keep me from the danger of an offended heart. When I face trials and difficulty, may I turn to you and not look away. Whatever I may feel in the moment, help me to trust you to bring me safely through such trials to your kingdom, no matter what. Amen.

* * *

VERSES 31-36

31 The One coming from above is above all things; the one of the earth is from the earth and speaks of earthly things. The One who comes from heaven is above all things.
32 That which He has seen and heard, to this He testifies, and no one receives His testimony.[15]

---

14. Brunson, "Don't Be Offended," 29-30.

15. Just as in the 1st century, many in our generation do not accept Jesus' testimony – concerning who He is or who God is. Jesus says as much to Nicodemus during their dialogue (see 3:11 above). Through His teaching and "signs," Jesus forces Nicodemus and

33 The one who accepts His testimony has certified[16] that God is true.
34 For the one whom God sent speaks the words of God, for He gives the Spirit without measure.[17]
35 The Father loves the Son and has given all things into His hand.
36 The one who believes in the Son has eternal life; but the one who disobeys the Son will not see life, and the wrath of God remains upon him."[18]

---

indeed every skeptic to confront several questions: namely, who is Jesus, are His claims about Himself true and what is my own response to Him?

16. The Greek verb here (ἐσφράγισεν, *esphragisen*) means literally to "set one's seal" or "certify" (as an official seal on a document) (BDAG, 980).

17. That is, since He is sent by God, the words Jesus speaks are God's. Christ's promise of an outpouring of the Holy Spirit at the end of verse references the Old Testament prophet Joel's vision of the Holy Spirit falling on all humanity ("And it shall come to pass afterward, that I will pour out my Spirit on all flesh" (Joel 2:28)). This takes place initially at Pentecost (Acts 2:33), and again among the believing gentiles following Peter's testimony at the centurion Cornelius' house at Caesarea (Acts 10:45).

Recall that when John the Baptist meets Jesus, he declares that he saw the Holy Spirit descending from heaven and remaining upon Him, and that God told him that Jesus baptizes not with water but with the Holy Spirit (1:32–33). It is in this sense that "[w]hereas God gave Old Testament prophets the Spirit by measure, He gave Him to Christ *without measure*. The Spirit was not in Christ as in a vessel, but as in a fountain . . . a bottomless ocean" (Henry, *Henry's Commentary*, 1522).

18. John doesn't record a further response from Nicodemus after his question "how can these things be?" in v.9. In effect, following Jesus' extended testimony about the necessity of and means to salvation, Nicodemus is left to ponder his incredulity, the choice between faith and disobedience, and the consequences of each. Nicodemus' later appearances in John's narrative, the first time questioning the Sanhedrin's right to pass judgment on Jesus without hearing His testimony (7:50–51), and the later when he brings a massive amount of costly myrrh and aloes to prepare Jesus' body for burial after the Crucifixion (19:39–40), suggest that he ultimately decided to believe in and follow Christ as Messiah.

4

John Chapter 4

VERSES 1-15

1 Now when Jesus learned that the Pharisees heard that Jesus was making and baptizing more disciples than John—
2 Although Jesus Himself was not baptizing but rather His disciples—
3 He left Judea and went again into Galilee.
4 And it was necessary for Him to pass through Samaria.[1]
5 So He came to a town of Samaria called Sychar, near the field that Jacob gave to his son Joseph.[2]
6 And Jacob's well was there. And Jesus being tired from the journey was sitting by the well; it was about the sixth hour.[3]
7 A woman of Samaria came to draw water. Jesus said to her, "Give me a drink";
8 For His disciples had gone into the city to buy food.

---

1. "Samaria lay between Judea in the south and Galilee in the north; anyone, therefore, who wished to go from Judea to Galilee 'had to pass through Samaria' unless he was prepared to make a detour through the Transjordan, with its largely Gentile population. Jesus on this occasion took the direct route from south to north" (Bruce, *Gospel of John*, 101).

2. The reference here is to Gen 28:22, where Jacob on his deathbed tells Joseph: "Moreover, I have given to you rather than to your brothers one mountain slope that I took from the hand of the Amorites with my sword and with my bow."

3. That is, around noon, at the beginning of the afternoon heat of the day.

9 Then the Samaritan woman said to Him, "How is it that you, being a Jew, ask me, a Samaritan woman, for a drink?"[4] For Jews do not associate with Samaritans.

10 Jesus answered and said to her, "If you knew the gift of God and who is the one saying to you, 'Give me a drink,' you would have asked Him and He would have given you living water."[5]

11 The woman said to Him, "Sir, you have no bucket to draw with and the well is deep; from where then do you have living water?

12 Are you greater than our father Jacob, who gave us the well and drank from it himself, along with his sons and their flocks?"

13 Jesus answered and said to her, "Everyone who drinks from this water will thirst again;

14 But whoever drinks from the water that I give to him will never thirst again, but the water that I will give to him will become in him a spring of water welling up to eternal life."

15 The woman says to Him, "Sir, give to me this water, so that I will not be thirsty or have to come here to draw."

* * *

REFLECTION: LIVING WATER

I love to get away to secluded stretches in the beautiful redwood forests covering the Bay and Pacific sides of the Santa Cruz Mountains near where Judith and I live. In my younger days I would do long trail runs. Now, I ride my gravel bike and on fire roads and single-track trails, the more remote the better. One key on that type of ride is to always be sure to carry enough water. The best is cool spring water, San Pellegrino or something similar.

But it's a fact that no matter how pure the water is, whether from the San Pellegrino spring or even if I drew from a sacred site like Jacob's well, I eventually grow thirsty and have to drink again.

---

4. The woman immediately recognizes the clear social boundaries and custom Jesus is "violating" and questions his reason(s) for doing so.

5. That is, the gift of God's grace in the form of eternal life through faith in Jesus the Messiah now come to earth. In John's era, "living water" would have been understood to mean water from a stream or running spring, as distinct from standing water drawn from a cistern. In Jer. 2:13, God calls Himself "the fountain of living waters," referring to fresh, running water representing His "all-sufficiency of grace and strength" (Henry, *Henry's Commentary*, 938; Bruce, *Gospel of John*, 104).

The same can be said of all the good things of earth that we come to "draw from" again and again for meaning and purpose in our lives, believing somehow that they will affirm and sustain us over the long term. Career, wealth, security of a home, one's spouse, circle of friends, fitness, good health, the list could go on...

But as Jesus shows the Samaritan woman at Jacob's well in Sychar, his living water of grace and life is the only water than can quench our inner soul-thirst. To paraphrase Tim Keller, we must not mistake good things in life for the ultimate things. Too often though we do just that, and consciously or unconsciously we try and turn "the good" into the ultimate source of meaning and purpose in our lives. When we do, no matter how good our object (be it career, a cause, even a loved one), being of this world it inevitably can't bear the weight of our expectations.

The well is indeed deep, and I need the living water of Christ himself, Christ alone.

If we draw from Jesus, the water of God's undying grace and faithful love is multiplied, becoming his life "welling up" in us when we sacrifice and use our gifts to bless and serve others.

PRAYER

Lord, I come again to draw at the well today. I come empty-handed, knowing also that the well is deep. Please give me your living water to drink, then use me to bless and encourage others. Amen.

*　　*　　*

VERSES 16-34

16 He said to her, "Go, call your husband and come here."
17 The woman answered and said to Him, "I do not have a husband." Jesus said to her, "You have spoken well in saying that 'I do not have a husband';
18 For you have had five husbands and he whom you have now is not your husband; this you have spoken truly."
19 The woman said to Him, "Sir, I perceive that you are a prophet.[6]

---

6. In words that may sound humorous to our jaded modern ears, the woman admits that her situation is indeed exactly as Jesus has described.

20 Our fathers worshiped on this mountain; and you say that in Jerusalem is the place where it is necessary to worship."[7]

21 Jesus said to her, "Believe Me, woman, the hour is coming when neither on this mountain nor in Jerusalem will you worship the Father.[8]

22 You worship what you do not know; we worship what we know, for salvation is from the Jews.[9]

23 But the hour is coming and now is, when true worshipers will worship the Father in spirit and in truth; for indeed the Father seeks worshipers such as these to worship Him.

24 God [is] spirit, and it is necessary for worshippers to worship Him in spirit and in truth."[10]

---

7. Caught by surprise and clearly embarrassed, the Samaritan woman attempts to direct the conversation away from her marital status by raising the theological issue of certain differences in beliefs between Samaritans and Jews. After the return of the Hebrew nation around 538 BC from the Babylonian captivity, relations between the Jews and Samaritans had grown increasingly acrimonious, and by John's and Jesus' day had reached the point of overt antagonism if not hatred (Bernard, *Exegetical Commentary*, 1:145).

"This mountain" in v21 is a reference to Mount Gerizim, at the foot of which Jacob's well is located. The Samaritan Pentateuch records the setting up of an altar on Mount Gerizim (the conventional reading being Mount Ebal). A Samaritan temple on Mount Gerizim is also recorded in the Jewish historian Josephus, and was reportedly destroyed by the Hasmonean leader John Hyrcanus during his reign (135–103 BC) (ESV study note). (Descendants of the Maccabee family, the Hasmonean dynasty ruled Judea and surrounding regions from 140–37 BC.)

8. In the Greek text, "you" here is in the plural, meaning "you the Samaritans." Jesus makes clear that ancient rivalries between Jews and Samaritans will become irrelevant when the true religion of the Gospel is fully realized, and every believer has become a living temple indwelt by the Holy Spirit (ESV study note).

9. Contrary to the Samaritan woman's assertion, Jesus' point here is that the key theological difference between the Jews and Samaritans is not *where* they worship but their understanding of *who* they worship. The Samaritans accepted the LORD as revealed in the Mosaic law as the one true God, but knew little about his person or character, since they rejected the Psalms and the Prophets as holy Scripture (the Samaritan Torah includes only the Pentateuch as its biblical canon) (Bernard, *Exegetical Commentary*, 1:147; Wikipedia, "Samaritan Pentateuch").

10. In explaining this verse, Henry cites Phil 3:3: "For we are the circumcision, who worship by the Spirit of God and glory in Jesus Christ and put no confidence in the flesh" and comments: "It is required of all that worship God that they worship Him *in spirit and in truth*. We must worship God *in spirit* [citing Phil 3:3]. We must depend on *God's Spirit* for strength and assistance. We must worship Him with fixedness of thought and a flame of affection, *with all that is within us. In truth*, that is, *in sincerity*. We must mind the power more than the form" (Henry, *Henry's Commentary*, 1525).

25 The woman said to Him, "I know that Messiah is coming, the One called Christ; when he comes, he will make known all things to us."
26 Jesus said to her, "I AM [He], the One speaking to you."

27 Just then His disciples came and marveled that He was speaking with a woman;[11] but no one actually said, "What are you seeking?" or "Why are you speaking with her?"
28 Then the woman left her water jar and went away into the city and said to the people,
29 "Come, behold a man said to me all the things that I ever did, is this not the Messiah?"
30 They [the people] went out from the city and were coming to Him.
31 Meanwhile the disciples were urging Him saying, "Rabbi, eat."
32 And He said to them, "I have food to eat that you do not know."
33 Then the disciples were saying to one another, "Surely no one brought Him [something] to eat?"
34 Jesus said to them, "My food is to do the will of the Him who sent Me and that I might finish His work."

* * *

REFLECTION: "MY FOOD"

Consider the "food" Jesus mentions in contrast to the food the disciples bring from the Samaritan village. Jesus' food, the bread of Heaven, is doing the will of the Father, teaching and saving the lost, inaugurating God's kingdom on earth, and in the process destroying the works of the devil (1 John 3:8).

Note the Savior's humility: Jesus describes the work as "his" (that is, God's) work, not "my" work.

What's your "food"?

PRAYER

Lord, thank you for the food you gave Jesus, and that he was so faithful to do the work you gave to him throughout his ministry on earth. Grant that we might recognize the precious bread from heaven that our Savior offers. We also have work to do in heaven's name. Help us to see that work as yours, not our own. Let us partake of Jesus' food every day, for the tuning of our hearts to the service of others. In Your Name, Amen.

---

11. For the custom of his day, it was scandalous that Jesus was speaking alone with a woman, and a Samaritan woman at that.

The Gospel of John

* * *

VERSES 35–54

35 "Do you not say 'It is yet four months and the harvest comes'? Behold I say to you, lift up your eyes and see the fields are white for harvest. Already
36 the one reaping receives a reward and gathers fruit for eternal life, so that the one sowing and the one reaping rejoice together. [12]
37 For in this the word is true that one sows and another reaps. [13]
38 I sent you to reap that for which you have not worked; others have worked and you have entered into their labor."
39 Many Samaritans from that town believed in Him because of the woman's testimony that "He told me everything that I ever did."
40 Then when the Samaritans came to Him, they were asking Him to stay with them; and He stayed there for two days.
41 And many more believed because of His word,
42 And they said to the woman that, "No longer on account of what you said do we believe, for we ourselves have heard and we know that He is truly the savior of the world."[14]

43 And after two days, he went from there into Galilee;
44 For Jesus Himself had testified that a prophet has no honor in his own hometown.
45 Then when He went into Galilee, the Galileans welcomed Him, having seen all the things which He did in Jerusalem at the festival, for they also went to the festival.

---

12. The verb is συνάγω (*sunago*), the same verb denoting the gathering together of God's people, and from which comes our English word "synagogue." The harvest of the gospel by Paul and other loyal disciples in the early church produces new communities of faith, the fruit of gospel seeds planted in Jesus' name and nourished against all odds by prayer and by the Holy Spirit.

13. Jesus makes two points with the agricultural metaphor of the reaper and the sower: first, that the work of both the sower and the reaper are necessary if there is to be a harvest, and the sower and reaper may not be the same person. Second, that the disciples must learn to harvest the crop of believers even though they may not have sowed the seed. *See* Bruce, *Gospel of John*, 114; and Brown, *According to John*, 38.

14. Having heard the woman's witness, the Samaritans at Sychar now see and hear for themselves that Jesus was not only "a prophet" (4:19), but the long-prophesied Messiah now come to earth in the flesh (4:25).

John Chapter 4

46 Then He went again to Cana of Galilee, where He had made the water wine.

And there was a certain royal official whose son was sick at Capernaum.[15]

47 Hearing that Jesus had come from Judea into Galilee he went to Him and begged that He might come down and heal his son, for he was about to die.

48 Jesus then said to him, "Unless you behold signs and wonders, you do not believe."

49 The royal official said to Him, "Sir, come down before my child dies."

50 Jesus said to him, "Go, your son lives." The man believed the word that Jesus spoke to him and went on us his way.[16]

51 And while was going down his servants met him saying that his son was alive.[17]

52 Then he asked them from what hour he began to get better; then told him that, "Yesterday at the seventh hour the fever left him."

53 The father then knew that it was at that hour Jesus said to him, "Your son lives," and he and his entire household believed.[18]

54 This was now the second sign that Jesus did when He came from Judea into Galilee.[19]

---

15. The Greek term John uses in describing the man's office, βασιλικὸς (*basilikos*), suggests that he was in the service of a king (*basileus*), likely Herod Antipas who was tetrarch of Galilee from 4 BC to 39 AD) (Carson, *According to John*, 238).

16. The "you" in this sentence is again plural. This suggests that Jesus is challenging not only the royal official but the Galilean people for focusing only on the "signs and wonders" rather than on the one doing them, and faith in him as Messiah (ESV). At the same time, Jesus shows mercy when the official begs him to "come down" (to Capernaum) to save his son. The ruler then takes Jesus at His word and goes on his way as Jesus tells him, showing that he, unlike most Galileans, is not simply entranced by the signs and wonders themselves (Carson, *According to John*, 239).

17. Jesus' word to the official proves true. The Son of God upholds the universe and all creatures in it "by the word of His power" (Heb 1:3).

18. Jesus by the merciful "word of His power" produces not only physical healing for the boy, but salvation for the official's entire household.

19. Jesus' "sign" of healing of the ruler's son follows the miracle of his turning the water into wine at the wedding in Cana (2:11).

5

John Chapter 5

VERSES 1-10

1 After this there was a feast of the Jews and Jesus went up to Jerusalem.[1]
2 Now in Jerusalem by the Sheep Gate there is a pool which in Hebrew or Aramaic is called Bethesda, which has five porticos.
3 In these were lying a multitude of invalids, the blind, the lame and the paralyzed.
5 And there was a certain man there who had been ill for thirty-eight years;
6 Jesus, seeing him lying there and knowing that he had already been there a long time,[2] said to him, "Do you want to be made well?"
7 The invalid answered Him, "Lord, I have no one to put me into the pool when the water is stirred; while I am going, another goes down before me."
8 Jesus said to him, "Take up your mat and walk."
9 And immediately the man was healed, and took up his mat and walked. And that day was a Sabbath.

---

1. With chapter 5, John begins a series of stories in which Jesus' miracles occur within the context of four Jewish feasts: this unnamed festival here in chapter 5, Passover (ch. 6), the Feast of Tabernacles (Succoth, ch. 7) and the Feast of Dedication (Hanukkah, ch. 10). The festival in ch. 5 is not named. Rather, what is important is that the miracle of healing that Jesus performs at the Bethesda pool (the third of Jesus' miraculous signs) occurs on the Sabbath. The fact that the healing takes place on the Sabbath is what triggers controversy with the Jewish leaders in Jerusalem about Jesus supposedly 'doing work' on the Sabbath.

2. That is, a long time in the condition of his affliction, seemingly without hope and certainly without a healer. Jesus sees the man in his need.

John Chapter 5

10 Then the Jews were saying to the one who had been healed, "It is the Sabbath, and it is not lawful for you to carry your mat."

*   *   *

REFLECTION: "TAKE UP YOUR MAT"

Jesus' simple command to the paralyzed man and his order's effect testify powerfully to this Sabbath healing. Given the Sabbath, the Jewish religious leaders unfortunately seek a pretext to beat back the challenge to their authority that Jesus and His ministry represent – an alleged violation of Sabbath rules against "working" (in this case, the former paralytic's carrying his mat [5:10]).

But Jesus' healing power is not bounded by religious conventions, including Levitical Sabbath restrictions on what is understood to constitute "labor." God's focus through Jesus is rather to have the man wholly healed, even if it means ostensibly breaking the Sabbath rule against work.

In the process, the mat that once marked the *de facto* boundary of the paralytic's world (since he could not move in his own power beyond it), he now carries as he walks, liberated from the former chains of his paralysis. The mat is now just a possession, no longer a border or barrier defining the limit of his world. Jesus' command sets him free.

I'm not aware of any instance in the Gospels of Jesus refusing to heal someone who asks for his help. To the contrary, he promises that "whoever comes to me I will never cast out" (6:37).

In my mind's eye, if I met Jesus in the street and asked for his healing from the cancer, I'm confident he would stop, look at me with loving mercy and say, "Go and be well." And so the fact that to date I've not received such an answer through prayer to the latest reoccurrence of my cancer is hard to understand and accept.

Psalm 43:5 says:

> "Why are you cast down, O my soul,
> And why are you in turmoil within me?
> Hope in God; for I shall again praise, my salvation and my God."

In Hebrew, the imperative command translated as "hope" here comes from the root יחל (*yahal*), which also means "to wait." And it seems fitting that the proper, fullest sense of the charge Jesus quoting the psalm gives us here is not only to *hope in* God but also as we do so, to *wait for* God. He knows not only the future but also much better than I do what is best. "Not my will, but Thy will be done."

> In this season, I do a fair amount of hoping and waiting. It is often neither pleasant nor easy, and I often chafe against it, or feel too tired to keep up the fight. But this is what I have to go on. "Hoping" means expecting the good, and "waiting" means trusting the Lord to provide it in the form and time that *he* chooses. And that is how I go on with God, one day at a time.
>
> PRAYER
>
> Lord, thank you for this witness that your merciful healing transcends every boundary and limit. Grant to us such healing in our hours of need. Amen!

*   *   *

VERSES 11–21

11 He answered them, "The One who made me well, He said to me, 'Take up your mat and walk.'"
12 They asked him, "Who is the man who said to you, 'Take up and walk?'"
13 The one who had been healed did not know who it was, for Jesus had withdrawn, as there was a crowd in the place.
14 After these things Jesus found him in the temple and said to him, "Behold, you have become well; sin no more, so that nothing worse should happen to you."[3]
15 The man went away and told the Jews that it was Jesus who made him well.
16 And because of this the Jews all the more were seeking to kill Jesus, because He was doing these things on the Sabbath.
17 But Jesus answered them, "My Father is working until now, and I am working";[4]
18 Therefore on account of this the Jews were seeking all the more to kill Jesus, because not only was He breaking the Sabbath, but also because He was calling God His own Father making Himself equal to God.

---

3. Jesus' admonition for the man to "sin no more" implies that in this case the man's disability had resulted from his own sin, and Jesus wanted him to know that he knew this (Bruce, *Gospel of John*, 126). This does not mean, however, that all personal ailments or suffering are due to sin (see John 9:2) (ESV).

4. Jesus teaches here that God "my Father" continues his redemption work on the Sabbath, and this is also the reason Jesus himself works, doing the redemption work of healing. Jesus' authority to "work" as God's Son transcends Levitical Sabbath regulation. The Pharisees' opposition to Jesus' authority (and identity) now begins in earnest.

19 Then Jesus answered and said to them, "Truly, truly I say to you, the Son is not able to do anything except what He sees the Father doing; for whatever He does, these things also the Son likewise does.
20 For the Father loves the Son and shows Him everything that He is doing, and He will show Him greater works than these, so that you may marvel. [5]
21 For just as the Father raises up the dead and gives them life, so also the Son gives life to whose whom He wishes."

* * *

REFLECTION: JUST AS THE FATHER GIVES LIFE, SO DOES THE SON

In Jewish tradition, which may extend to pre-Christian times, the second of the eighteen benedictions addressing God in the great synagogue prayer known as the *Amidah* says the following:

> "Thou, O *Lord*, art mighty forever; thou quickenest the dead; though art mighty to save.
> Thou sustaineth the living with loving-kindness, thou quickenest the dead in great mercy, thou supportest the fallen, healest the sick, loosest those who are bound, and keepest faith with those who sleep in the dust.
> Who is like Thee, O *Lord* of mighty acts?
> Who is comparable to Thee, O King, who bringest to death and quickenest again, and causes salvation to spring forth?
> Yea, thou art faithful to quicken the dead!
> Blessed art Thou, O *Lord*, who quickenest the dead!"

The prayer reflects Jewish belief that only God can raise the dead. Against this background, as he answers the Pharisees, Jesus doesn't claim to be God's earthly instrument for restoring life, as Elijah and Elisha were. He claims for himself as God's Son "the divine prerogative of restoring life"[6].

Jesus is the wellspring of life, and its restorer.

PRAYER

Lord Jesus, thank you for raising Lazarus, and by that testimony affirming that you have the power and authority to raise up all who call on your name. Only you can restore the life that we need. May we see and know your resurrection power firsthand. In your name, Amen.

---

5. "You" here is again plural as Jesus addresses the Jewish religious establishment collectively. The following verse (5:21) seems to clearly anticipate Jesus' last and greatest "sign" before his own resurrection, the raising of Lazarus.

6. Bruce, *Gospel of John*, 129.

The Gospel of John

* * *

VERSES 22-47

22 For the Father judges no one but has given all judgment to the Son,
23 So that all might honor the Son as they honor the Father. For the one not honoring the Son does not honor the Father who sent Him.[7]
24 Truly, truly I say to you that the one hearing My word and believing the One who sent me has eternal life and does not come unto judgment, but has passed over from death into life.
25 Truly, truly I say to you that the hour comes and now is when the dead will hear the voice of the Son of God and those who hear will live.
26 For just as the Father has life in Himself, so also He has given to the Son to have in Himself.
27 And He gave Him authority to pass judgment, because He is the Son of Man.[8]
28 Do not marvel[9] at this, because the hour is coming in which all those in the tombs will hear His voice and will come out,
29 Those who have done good unto the resurrection of life and who have done evil unto the resurrection of judgment.

---

7. Jesus' point here is that the Jewish religious leaders are in effect dishonoring God by not honoring Christ himself (and his message), having been sent by God.

8. The very works that Jewish faith recognized God does on the Sabbath—giving life and judging—are precisely the ones that Jesus declares here the Father has entrusted to him (Brown, *According to John*, 41).

Jesus' words call to mind Dan 7:13-14's magisterial vision of Christ's eternal reign as the Son of Man. As Daniel foretold, Jesus' kingdom has come, and shall not pass away:

> "I saw in the night visions,
> And behold, with the clouds of heaven,
> There came one like a son of man
> And He came to the Ancient of Days
> And was presented before Him.
> And to Him was given dominion and glory and a kingdom,
> That all peoples, nations and languages should serve Him;
> His dominion is an everlasting dominion,
> Which shall not pass away,
> And His kingdom one
> That shall not be destroyed."

9. The plural form of the verb here, "Do not [you] marvel," reflects that Jesus is continuing to admonish the same Jewish leaders who took issue with his healing of the crippled man by the Pool of Siloam.

John Chapter 5

30 I am not able to do anything from Myself; just as I hear I judge, and my judgement is righteous, because I do not seek My will but the will of the Him who sent Me.

31 If I bear witness concerning Myself, My testimony is not true;
32 But another is bearing witness concerning Me, and I know that the testimony He makes concerning Me is true.[10]
33 You have sent to John, and he has testified[11] to the truth;
34 I do not receive testimony from man, but I am saying these things so that you might be saved.[12]
35 He was the bright and shining lamp, and you were willing to rejoice for a time in his light.[13]
36 But I have the testimony greater than John; for the works that the Father has given me so that I might complete them, these works that I do testify concerning Me that the Father has sent me.[14]
37 And the Father who sent Me, He has testified concerning Me. You have never heard His voice nor have you seen His form.
38 And His word you do not have abiding in you, because the One that He sent, in Him you do not believe.
39 You search the Scriptures, because you believe in them you have eternal life; and it is they that bear witness about Me;
40 But you do not wish to come to Me that you might have life.
41 I do not accept glory from man,

---

10. According to the Torah (Deut 19:15) and Rabbinical schools, the testimony of at least two witnesses was necessary to establishment any matter of fact in a criminal or other case of wrongdoing (Bernard, *Exegetical Commentary*, 1:247).

11. The perfect tense of the verb in the original Greek here attests to the now-completed nature of John the Baptist's ministry and witness in the Transjordan regarding Jesus and his coming as Messiah.

12. Notice Jesus' desire to save even those seeking to kill him, using the Spirit's witness to his identity and purpose in coming to bring salvation to all who would receive it.

13. Note the careful and important distinction John draws between the light-bearer, or "lamp," namely John the Baptist, and the light that he bears or shows—that is, Jesus. When John (the disciple) first mentions John the Baptist, he is careful to point out that John "was not the light, but came to bear testimony of the light" (John 1:8). The purpose a lamp is to show the light it bears, burning brightly and illuminating all around. John discharges his duty faithfully and well (Bruce, *Gospel of John*, 135).

14. That is, by doing the works that God gave him to do, Jesus shows himself to be the Son of God (Fee, *How to Read the Bible*, 135). The "signs" that Jesus does testify that he is sent as Messiah, from the Father. John the Baptist's ministry thus both anticipates and announces the Messiah's coming unto Israel.

42 But I have known you, that you do not have the love of God in you.[15]

43 I have come in the name of My Father, and you do not receive Me; but if another comes in his own name, that one you will receive.

44 How can you believe receiving glory from one another, but the glory from the only God you do not seek?

45 Do not suppose that I will accuse you before the Father. The one accusing you is Moses, in whom you have hoped.[16]

46 For if you believed in Moses, you would believe in Me; for he wrote about Me.[17]

47 And if you do not believe his writings, how will you believe My words?"

* * *

REFLECTION: JESUS' THREE-FOLD WITNESS

Jesus cites three sources to corroborate his testimony about himself:

- First, the works God has sent him to complete on earth testify concerning him, that the Father has sent him (5:36);
- Second, God the Father himself "has testified" concerning Jesus (the Greek perfect verb form here indicating completed action), even though the Jewish religious leaders have never heard his voice or seen his form (5:37); and
- Lastly, the Scriptures given to Israel themselves testify to Jesus' identity and advent as Messiah (5:38).

Jesus adduces this three-fold witness to meet the requirements of Jewish law noted above (see n.91) that there by at least two reliable witnesses in order to establish 'valid testimony.' Jesus offers three: God himself, Jesus' own works and the holy scriptures themselves. (Interestingly, as a further witness, the

---

15. Recall John's pointed observation earlier that Jesus "knew what was in man" (2:25).

16. Jesus in his incarnation has come to save, not to judge the world (John 3:17, 12:45). The later judgment God has given Jesus will be executed at the Second Coming at the end of the age.

17. The one now standing in witness against the Jews' unbelief is none other than Moses, who Jesus declares "wrote of me" as the prophet to come who will speak to the Hebrews all that the Lord commands him to say (see Deut 18:15–19). Jesus here is repeating his earlier assertion that the Jewish scriptures all testify concerning him (see 5:39). Collectively, such verses constitute the basis—Christ's own word—for Christians to read the Tanakh christologically. Admonishing Jewish worshippers in Solomon's Portico at the Temple in Jerusalem, Peter echoes Jesus' declaration in Acts 3:22–26 as he quotes Deut 18:15 to show that Jesus was in fact "the prophet like me" promised by Moses whom God would raise up "from among" the Hebrew nation.

Holy Spirit also testifies to Jesus' divine nature as the figure of the dove alights on him during his baptism by John (1:29–34).

Consider these blessed witnesses, and the Lord's question to his disciples, and to all across the ages who would follow him: "Who do you say that I am?" (Mark 8:29).

What is your answer?

*   *   *

6

John Chapter 6

VERSES 1-15

1 After this Jesus went away across the Sea of Galilee, of Tiberias.¹
2 And a large crowd was following Him, because they were seeing the signs that He was doing on the sick.²
3 And Jesus went up on the mountain and sat down there with His disciples.
4 And it was near the Passover, the feast of the Jews.³

    1. As chapter six opens, the scene seems to shift abruptly from Jerusalem to Galilee. But in fact, some time has passed between Jesus' declamation to the Jewish religious leaders after he healed the paralytic man at the Siloam Pool in Jerusalem and his journey now across the Sea of Galilee.

    2. What motivated this great crowd to follow Jesus? John indicates here that the crowd's motivation was merely to see the spectacle of "the signs" that Jesus was doing upon those who were sick, rather than experience his teaching or healing for themselves. In Matt 11:7, when Jesus speaks to the crowds following him about John the Baptist, he asks, "What did go into the wilderness to see?" Jesus then identifies John the Baptist as "Elijah who is to come" (Matt 13:14) who will prepare the way for Messiah (Mal 3:1, 4:5). Neither the Jewish leaders who went to question John the Baptist in the Transjordan, nor the crowd following Jesus in eastern Galilee seem to recognize either the messenger or the Messiah himself.

    3. John's mention of the Passover here is not merely incidental and raises several questions:

    First, this is the only time when John's Gospel records Jesus as being anywhere other than in Jerusalem during the season of Passover. The first Passover mentioned in John's account finds Jesus cleansing the Temple (2:13), while the last is at His death (13:1). Why is Jesus this time here in Galilee, when every other Jew with the means to do so has made the pilgrimage to celebrate the festival in Jerusalem? We discover the answer shortly, in

5 Then lifting up His eyes and seeing that a great crowd was coming to Him Jesus said to Philip, "Where will we buy bread so that these may eat?"
6 And He was saying this to test him, for He knew what He was about to do.[4]
7 Philip answered Him, "Two hundred denarii of bread would not be enough that each of these might receive a little."
8 One of His disciples, Andrew the brother of Simon Peter, said to Him,
9 "There is a boy here who has seven barley loaves and two small fishes; but what is this for so many?"
10 Jesus said, "Have the people sit down." There was much grass in the place. Then the men sat down, about five thousand in number.
11 Jesus then took the loaves and after giving thanks distributed them to those reclining and likewise the fish, as much as they wanted.
12 And when they were full, He said to His disciples, "gather together the leftover pieces, so that nothing is lost."
13 Then they gathered up and filled twelve baskets of pieces from the five barley loaves that were left over by those who had eaten.[5]
14 Then the people beholding the sign that He did were saying, "This is truly the Prophet who is coming into the world."
15 Then Jesus, knowing that they were about to come and seize Him to make Him king, again withdrew to the mountain by Himself.

---

the next "sign" that Jesus performs as he feeds the five thousand.

Second, why does John bother to mention the Passover to begin with? Again, the answer to this second question comes later in the chapter, in Jesus' I AM statements identifying himself as the "Bread of Life" (6:35) and the "Living Bread coming down from heaven" (6:51). With these statements Jesus declares himself as God's true 'bread that satisfies forever' while distinguishing himself from the manna from heaven given in Sinai through the ministry of Moses that was given daily but also perished daily. Jesus is the true bread of heaven given once and for all, and who abides for all eternity.

4. Jesus' question intentionally confronts the ever practically-minded Phillip with the seeming impossibility of the situation. This miracle's confluence with the Passover is a hint of its importance: the feeding of the five thousand is the only one of Jesus' miracles recorded in all four Gospel accounts. Note also that while John mentions only the men in attendance; including women and children, the total number of people that were fed may have been closer to twenty thousand (Carson, *According to John*, 270).

5. John emphasizes the bounty Jesus generates from the seemingly small contribution offered to him by the boy, and which he has committed to God. What does the Scripture teach us from this? Perhaps the boy offering up the loaves and fish had greater faith than Jesus' disciples!

Twelve baskets signifies both the completeness of the nation of Israel, echoing earlier biblical imagery (Wellman, "What Does The Number Twelve (12) Mean or Represent in the Bible"), and implies one basket's worth may have been gathered up by each disciple.

* * *

REFLECTION: "BUT WHAT IS THIS FOR SO MANY?"

Andrew's question is the one that many of the "practically minded" among us no doubt might ask, confronted with similar circumstances.

An urgent need presents itself. Jesus asks a testing question. Realist Phillip realizes immediately the sheer scale of the crowd's need for a meal in this area "on the far side" of the Sea of Galilee and the impossibility of the situation. He reminds Jesus (as if the Lord wasn't already aware!) that the sum of eight months' wages wouldn't be enough to feed such a massive crowd.

Then Andrew notices what the boy standing nearby has, a pittance weighed against the need of the moment. John records nothing of the lad's willingness to share his modest meal.

But from this difficult reality Jesus makes his miracle, the fourth of seven miraculous "signs" described in John's Gospel. Note that Jesus gives no teaching beforehand. Instead, John just recounts the simple action of what follows: something is available. Somehow, the boy is willing to surrender his lunch to Jesus. Jesus gives thanks to God and, as he does at the Last Supper, distributes the bread (together with the fish), and commands his disciples to gather up the abundance that is left over afterward.

The details of this "sign" echo a miracle Elisha performs that also reveals God's faithful provision (see 2 Kgs 4:42–44)[6]. But Jesus' sign also points to an event in Israel's more distant past, centered in the Sinai, as well as forward to the Last Supper. Jesus identifies himself as the real manna prefigured in God's daily provision for Israel while they sojourn in Sinai. That is, the bread that Jesus consecrates this Passover on the Galilean mountainside anticipates the new manna of his body and blood given at the Last Supper and literally poured out for humanity on the summit of Golgotha in Jerusalem at the next year's Passover.

I AM the One who comes walking on the water, Jesus shows his disciples later that night. *Do not fear.*

I AM the Bread of Life, he will soon declare in the synagogue at Capernaum (6:35), *coming down out of heaven and given for the life of the world. Feed on me. I lose none of those whom the Father has given me, but will raise them up on the last day* (6:39).

This "sign" shows us that only in Jesus and his broken and consecrated body and blood do we find our true sustenance and inspiration. Jesus is my

---

6. Brown, *According to John*, 41–42.

manna. I need him to live. The crowd following him from the far side of the Sea of Galilee back to Capernaum believed their need was satisfied because their stomachs were full. This sign in fact points to something infinitely better—the miracle of Calvary, Jesus' sacrifice of himself for the life of the world and victory over sin and death.

PRAYER

Lord, keep us from the same mistake in seeking our "bread of life" from earthly goods that cannot satisfy. What might you do with my modest gift offered in faith to you today?

Thank you for the miraculous sign on the mountainside, and the new manna that Jesus is your precious body and blood, and for your promise to raise up us on the last day. May every person reading this find their refuge in you, our Messiah and faithful shepherd.

In your name, Amen.

*　　*　　*

VERSES 16–35

16 When evening came, His disciples went down to the sea
17 And getting into a boat they went across the sea to Capernaum. It was now dark and Jesus had not yet come to them,
18 The sea became rough because a strong wind was blowing.
19 Then after having rowed about twenty-five or thirty stadia they saw Jesus walking on the sea and coming near the boat, and they were afraid.[7]
20 And He said to them, *"It is I. Do not fear."*[8]
21 So they were glad to take Him into the boat, and immediately the boat reached the shore where they were going.
22 The next day the crowd that was standing on the other side of the sea saw that there had been no other boat there but one and that Jesus had not gone with His disciples in the boat but His disciples had departed alone.

---

7. One *stadia* is about one-eighth of a mile, so the boat had gone three to four miles (ESV study note). Note the compounding of the disciples' fear—fear of the storm itself coupled with the shock of seeing Jesus walking on the water, the fifth of his miraculous signs.

8. Literally in the Greek, Jesus is saying, "I AM," the same words that God uses to identify himself in Exod 3:14 ("I AM WHO I AM").

23 Other boats came from Tiberias near to the place where they had eaten the bread after the Lord had given thanks.[9]

24 When the crowd saw that neither Jesus nor His disciples were there, they embarked in the boats and went to Capernaum seeking Jesus.

25 And finding Him on the other side of the sea they said to Him, "Rabbi, when did You come here?"

26 Jesus answered them and said, "Truly, truly I say to you, you seek Me not because you saw signs, but because you ate of the loaves and were satisfied.[10]

27 Do not work for food that is perishing but rather for the food that remains unto eternal life, which the Son of Man will give to you; for on Him God the Father has set His seal."[11]

28 Then they said to Him, "What should we do that we might do the works of God?"

29 Jesus answered and said to them, "This is the work of God, that you might believe in the One whom He sent."[12]

30 Then they said to Him, "Then what sign are you doing, so that we may see it and believe in you? What work are you doing?

31 Our fathers ate manna in the desert, as it is written, 'Bread from heaven He gave them to eat.'"[13]

---

9. That is, on the eastern shore of the Sea of Galilee where Jesus had fed the crowd of five thousand men along with women and children on the mountainside.

10. Many in the crowd were just looking for a free meal if they could get one. Would a large crowd following Jesus today be different?

11. In first century Israel, the sealing of document with wax or clay signified either ownership or authentication (ESV study note). John's point here is that Jesus is the One whom God has appointed as his certified and authorized agent to bestow his life-giving food for the world (Bruce, *Gospel of John*, 151). If the aorist past sense of the verb in the Greek here suggests that we identify Jesus' "sealing" with a single past event, "we should probably think of our Lord's baptism" (Bruce, *Gospel of John*, 152; see also Carson, *According to John*, 284).

12. Note his questioners' focus on "doing" (humanity ever ready then as now with its works checklist), and Jesus' response focusing on being/believing.

13. The most explicit reference from the Hebrew Scriptures appears to be Ps 78:23–24:

"Yet He commanded the skies above and opened the doors of heaven,
And He rained down on them manna to eat, and gave them the grain of heaven."

Also implicated in John's reference to "eating manna in the desert" are (i) the "manna" linking the exodus (the manna God gives the people in the Sinai wilderness) with the Passover's unleavened bread, (ii) the characterization of Jesus as the prophet promised by Moses (Deut 18:15) and (iii) the messianic hope that God would again provide manna for his people during Rome's occupation of the Kingdom of Israel (ESV study note).

John Chapter 6

32 Jesus said to them, "Truly truly I say to you, Moses did not give you the bread from heaven, but my Father will give to you true bread from heaven; 33 For the Bread of God is the One coming down out of heaven and giving life to the world."
34 Then they said to Him, "Lord, give us this bread always."
35 Jesus said to them, "I AM the Bread of Life; the one who comes to Me will never hunger, and the one believing in Me will never thirst." [14]

* * *

REFLECTION: BREAD OF LIFE FROM THE HOUSE OF BREAD

"Bethlehem" in Hebrew means literally "house of bread" (בֵּית לֶחֶם). The prophet Micah writes this of the hometown of Jesse, King David's father:

> "But you, O Bethlehem Ephrathah, who are too little to be among the clans of Judah,
> From you shall come forth for me One who is to be ruler in Israel,
> Whose coming forth is from of old, from ancient days" (Micah 5:2).

> "道成了肉身、住在我們中間、充充滿滿的有恩典有真理"
> "The Word became bodily flesh, and dwelt among us, full of grace and truth" (John 1:14).

Christmas celebrates the Messiah becoming human. He comes to earth at Bethlehem, the House of Bread, bringing for us his own body as the Bread of Life, later to be broken for our salvation:

> "... the Lord Jesus on the night when He was betrayed took bread,
> And when He had given thanks, He broke it, saying,
> 'This is My body, which is for you. Do this in remembrance of Me'" (1 Cor 11:23–24).

14. In this, the first of his seven "I AM" declarations in John's gospel, Jesus' point is that the loaves and fishes that the crowd had eaten on the mountainside were like "the manna which Israel ate in the days of Moses"—that is, "material food, even though it came by the will of God. But there is another kind of bread which comes down from heaven—true, real bread sustaining the inmost and most lasting life of men and women" (Bruce, *Gospel of John*, 152). Jesus is saying here that *he is the new manna* available to those believing in him. Unlike the manna in the desert which appeared miraculously but perished by the next day and had no power to save those it fed from death, Jesus is the true bread who provides, and abides with, all who love and trust in Him, for all eternity. This is possible only by the miracle of his cruciform death and resurrection.

Gabriel tells Mary "the Holy Spirit will come upon you, and the power of the Most High will overshadow you; therefore the one to be born will be called holy, the Son of God" (Luke 1:35).

The profound mystery of the incarnation perhaps explains our culture's tendency to view Christmas simplistically.

The consumerist manner that we in the US celebrate Christmas makes it all too easy to either trivialize or completely overlook the complex and difficult circumstances in which the Incarnation took place.

- Consider Mary's physical and emotional ordeal as she accompanied Joseph on the multi-day journey for tax registration from Nazareth to Bethlehem while being nine months pregnant.
- Yes, the angel of the Lord announces to the shepherds "good news of great joy for all the people" (Luke 2:10). Yet it's also true that Jesus is born under a paranoid tyrant who in a later attempt to murder him visits slaughter and mourning upon his hometown, fulfilling the elegiac prophecy from Jer 31 quoted early on in Luke's Gospel: "A voice was heard in Ramah, weeping and loud lamentation, Rachel weeping for her children; she refused to be comforted, because they are no more" (Luke 2:18).
- In a similar vein, when Jesus is presented at the temple in Jerusalem for circumcision on the eighth day after his birth, the pious Simeon gives Mary ominous news that her son is appointed "for a sign that is opposed ... thus the thoughts of many will be revealed," and tells her also that "a sword shall pierce your own soul also" (Luke 2:36).
- Finally, unvoiced in all the gospel accounts of Christmas is the question of what Joseph and Mary's relationship must have been like for each of them as they began life together as a family knowing their firstborn son is of God on High.

All the more miraculously then, God's message to us through the incarnation is that Jesus comes to all who humbly would receive him, as our faithful Messiah from the House of Bread, giving for us his own body as the new manna.

We seldom think of it this way, but it should not shock us that *Christmas is cruciform*. That is, the only way we can fully understand Bethlehem is to remember the Upper Room, the Last Supper, and Golgotha. "This is My body, which is given for you" (Luke 22:19). Jesus the Bread of Life is our spiritual food. Without him, our souls starve and we perish.

John Chapter 6

PRAYER

Lord Jesus, our Bread of Life from the House of Bread, thank you for coming for us as one of us, born amongst gentle animals in a lonely stable, close against a cold winter's night. Amen.
(written at Christmas, 2023)

* * *

VERSES 36–40

36 "But I say to you that have you have seen [Me] and yet you do not believe.
37 Everything that the Father gives to Me will come to Me, and the one who comes to Me I will never cast out,[15]
38 because I have come down from heaven not to do My will but the will of the One who sent Me.
39 And this is the will of the One who sent Me, that everything He has given to me I should not lose any of it; but I should raise it up on the last day.
40 For this is the will of My Father, that everyone beholding the Son and believing in Him should have eternal life; and I will raise him up on the last day."

* * *

REFLECTION: "I WILL RAISE HIM UP"

In John 6:40b the original Greek reads as follows:

> "οὗτο δὲ ἐστι τὸ θέλημα τοῦ πέμψαντός με, ἵνα πᾶς ὁ θεωρῶν τὸν υἱὸν καὶ πιστεύων εἰς αὐτὸν ἔχῃ ζωὴν αἰώνιον, **καὶ ἀναστήσω αὐτὸν ἐγὼ** τῇ ἐσχάτῃ ἡμέρᾳ."

In the literal phrasing of the Greek text, Jesus says, "I will raise him up, I."

Jesus in His mercy envelops us with His life, keeping us safe with him forever. "I have set the Lord always before me, because He is at my right hand, I shall not be shaken (Ps 16:8). The power of our Savior's undying and eternal love surrounds and protects us. "The life that was made manifest . . . the eternal life" (1 John 1:2) works to seal and raise up the life of every single person who beholds (that is, sees Jesus for who He truly is) and believes in Him.

---

15. All whom God gives to Jesus seek him. Jesus in turn never drives away, and always loves and accepts, those who come to him.

At its core, faith comes down to trust:

Do I trust in Christ's power to raise me up on the last day? Do I "behold" (beholding; θεωρια) Jesus with the eye of faith and believe this promise? Or do I just say those words on Sunday?

Pause for a few moments, and in the silence, recall everything Jesus has done for you already and is doing in your life now. Consider all that he wants to do for you in the future. Rest in your awareness of Jesus' work in you through the Holy Spirit.

Where does this awareness lead you? Perhaps to repentance, praise, petition or clarity about an action that you need to take or refrain from. Consider and pray accordingly, as you reflect.

PRAYER

Lord Jesus, thank you for the blessed light of the new morning you have made. May I experience your presence, peace and power in me throughout this day and rest peacefully when I lay down tonight. Abide with me. May I keep you always before me, as my light and my guide. In your name, Amen.

* * *

VERSES 41–59

41 Then the Jews were grumbling about Him because He said, "I AM the Bread coming down out of heaven,"
42 And they were saying, "Is this not Jesus the son of Joseph, whose father and mother we know? How now does He now say that, 'I have come down out of heaven?'"
43 Jesus answered and said to them, "Do not murmur with one another.
44 No one is able to come to Me unless the Father the One sending Me draws him, and I will raise him up on the last day.
45 It is written in the prophets, 'And they will all be taught by God'; everyone hearing from the Father and learning comes to Me.[16]
46 No one has seen the Father except the One with God, He has seen the Father.
47 Truly truly I say to you, the one believing has eternal life.
48 *I AM* the Bread of Life.

---

16. John here paraphrases the assurance given to Jerusalem in Isa 54:13: "All of your children shall be taught by the LORD, and great shall be the peace of your children" (ESV).

John Chapter 6

49 Your fathers ate the manna in the desert and they died;[17]

50 This is the Bread coming down out of heaven, that one may eat of it and not die.

51 I AM the Living Bread coming down from heaven; if anyone eats from this bread he will live forever, and the bread that I will give is My body [given] for the life of the world."[18]

52 Then the Jews were quarreling with one another saying, "How is he able to give to us his body to eat?"

53 Then Jesus said to them, "Truly truly I say to you, unless you eat the body of the Son of Man and drink His blood, you have no life in you.

54 The one who eats My flesh and drinks My blood has eternal life, and I will raise him on the last day.[19]

55 For My flesh is true food, and My blood is true drink.

56 The one who eats My flesh and drinks My blood abides in Me and I in him.

57 Just as the Living Father sent Me and I live through the Father, so also the one feeding on Me will live through Me.

58 This is the bread that came down from heaven, not as the fathers ate and died; the one eating this bread will live forever."

59 He said these things while teaching in the synagogue at Capernaum.

* * *

REFLECTION: BREAD, WATER AND LIGHT

With His "I AM" statement in John 6:51, Jesus reveals himself as the new Torah, the new manna, and the new Passover sacrifice with his body and blood:

> 17. For all of its miraculous properties, the manna given in Sinai could not impart eternal life. The wilderness generation who ate the manna in the desert died there (Bruce, *Gospel of John*, 157).
>
> 18. "The true sustenance and refreshment of our spiritual life are to be found only in Him who died that we might live. In all ways in which His people freed on Him by faith—not only at the Holy Table, but in reading and hearing the Word of God, or in private or united prayer and meditation (to mention no more)—they may fulfill the conditions which He lays down here, and receive the promised blessing" (Bruce, *Gospel of John*, 160).
>
> 19. Note Jesus' repeated emphasis on the certain eschatological promise of the ever-lasting life that he offers. This is his *fourth* mention (see previously 6:39, 40, 44) of raising up on the last day *all of those* given to him by God who sent him. The people saved are those who behold and believe in the Son as the One possessing eternal life. John's point here is that these believers are also the ones who partake of Jesus' flesh and his blood given for humanity.

"The rabbis said: if thine enemy hunger, feed him with the bread of the Torah.
Jesus said: I AM the living bread which came down from heaven (John 6:51).

The rabbis said: As water is life for the world, so also the words of the Torah are life for the world.
Jesus said: whoever drinks of the water that I will give him will never be thirsty again... If anyone thirsts, let Him come to me and drink. (John 4:14; 7:37).

The rabbis said: As oil is light for the world, so also are the words of the Torah light for the world.
Jesus said: I AM the light of the world; He who follows me will not walk in darkness, but will have the light of life (John 8:12).

What the rabbis ascribe to the Law, John testifies [is fulfilled only] in Jesus the Messiah, the living Word of God...
The law was given through Moses; grace and truth came through Jesus Christ (John 1:17)."[20]

Bread, water, and light—one might ask, how could Jesus be so many things at once? Only if we accept Christ's totalizing identity as the Son of God do his words, including his promises, make sense. In the I AM statements that John records, Jesus is recapitulating the message of the Tetragrammon for the divine name יְהוָה ("I AM who I AM") revealed to Moses in Exod 3:14. Messiah is telling us he is everything we need. It seems almost too good be true. God is my _____ [fill in the blank], and in Jesus Christ every promise of God is "yes"! (2 Cor 1:20).

We discover the gift of Jesus' body and blood first revealed here, at Capernaum, and then consummated on the Cross at Passover in Jerusalem the following year. This is Christ's light of illumination for the world, his deliverance for us from our sins and ourselves. Hallelujah!

* * *

VERSES 60–71

60 Then many of his disciples when they heard it said, "This is a hard word; who can hear it?"

61 Then Jesus perceiving in Himself that His disciples were grumbling[21] about this said to them, "Does this offend you?

---

20. Ellis, *World of St. John*, 26–27.

21. Note the Jews' grumbling in v. 41 and arguing in v. 52, and the disciples' own grumbling (the same Greek verb) in here in v. 61. The "word" or saying that Jesus gives

John Chapter 6

62 Then what if you should see the Son of Man ascending to where He was before?

63 It is the Spirit that gives life, the flesh accomplishes nothing. The words that I have spoken to you are spirit and they are life.

64 But there are some of you who do not believe." For Jesus knew from the beginning there were some who did not believe and who His betrayer was.

65 And He said, "For this reason I have told to you that no one is able to come to Me unless it were granted to him by the Father."

66 After this many of His disciples turned back and no longer walked with Him.

67 Then Jesus said to the Twelve, "Do you also want to go away?"

68 Simon Peter answered Him, "Lord, to whom should we go? You have the words of eternal life.

69 And we have believed and have come to know that You are the Holy One of God." [22]

70 Jesus answered them, "Have I not called you, the Twelve? But one of you is a devil."

71 He was speaking of Judas, son of Simon Iscariot; for he, one of the Twelve, was about to betray Him.

---

about the necessity of "feeding on" his body and blood and thereby to abide in him, was hard for many if not most in the synagogue and even his own disciples to hear.

22. As Jesus has just taught in 6:65, Peter's spiritual understanding of Jesus as the Messiah is given to him by God.

> "'The Holy One of God' appears as a messianic designation in Mark 1:24 (on the lips of a demon-possessed person, significantly enough) . . .
>
> If the words of Jesus were words of life, as the words of no other were, how could Peter or any one like-minded ever wish to leave this Master to follow someone else. Others might be disillusioned because Jesus, instead of fulfilling the expected messianic programme and leading a war of national liberation, insisted on the spiritual character of His kingdom . . .
>
> Others had been prepared to acknowledge Jesus as the second Moses, providing his people with food, but had no time for [His] living bread which was offered for the life of the world. Peter and his companions refused to be put off, but believed what He said . . .
>
> He was more than the prophet like Moses; He was the Holy One of God . . . Andrew had been more than right when he found his brother Simon and told him, 'We have found the Messiah (1:41). This was in truth 'the One of whom Moses in the law, and the prophets wrote' (1:45)'" (Bruce, *Gospel of John*, 165–66).

7

John Chapter 7

VERSES 1–53

1 After this Jesus walked about in Galilee. He did not wish to go about in Judea, because the Jews were seeking to kill Him.
2 It was near the time of the Jewish Feast of Tabernacles.[1]

---

1. Celebrated in September or October, *Sukkot* (חַג הַסֻּכּוֹת) is the feast of ingathering marking the end of the agricultural year, celebrated to this day in the Jewish calendar of high holidays. In Jesus' day, it was the festival around which the Jewish agrarian economy organized itself. By this time of year in the autumn cycle,

> "all of the harvests had been safely gathered in, not only the barley and wheat harvests, which were reaped between April and June, but the grape and olive harvests too. [It] was an occasion for great rejoicing (Exod 23:16, 34:22) . . . [and was called] the festival of booths (*sukkot*) because for the full week that it lasted, people lived in makeshift booths of branches and leaves waiting to enter the promised land; town-dwellers erected them in their courtyards or on their flat housetops. Many Jews from outlying parts of Palestine and from the Dispersion went to Jerusalem for the festival, for this was one of the three great pilgrimages of the Jewish year" (Bruce, *Gospel of John*, 170; Ellis, *World of St. John*, 69).

The other two were Passover (Pasach, or חַג הַפֶּסַח) and the Feast of Weeks (or Shavuot, שָׁבוּעוֹת), celebrating the wheat harvest, which Christians celebrate as Pentecost (Lev 23:15–23 "you shall count fifty days to the day after the seventh sabbath" (that is, 50 days after Passover); Acts 2:1ff.

The week of celebration during *Sukkot* was highlighted by two ceremonies in the temple, the water-pouring and illumination of the temple courts. Like Passover, this festival also pointed by the future when healing water would flow from a renewed temple (Ezek 47) and when "night shall be no more" (Zech 14:7; Rev 22:5) (Ellis, *World of St. John*, 69).

3 Then His brothers said to Him, "Depart from here and go into Judea, so that your disciples may see your works that you are doing;[2]

4 for no one who wishes to be openly known acts in secret. If you are doing these things, show yourself to the world."

5 For not even His own brothers believed in Him.

6 Then Jesus said to them, "My hour is not yet come, but your time is always ready.

7 The world cannot hate you, but it hates me, because I testify that its works are evil.[3]

8 You go up to the festival; I do not go up to this festival, because My hour is not yet fully come."

9 After saying this He remained in Galilee.

10 And after His brothers went up to the feast, then He also went up not openly but in secret.[4]

11 Then the Jews were looking for Him at the feast and were saying, "Where is He?"

12 And there was much murmuring concerning Him in the crowds; some were saying that, "He is good" but others were saying, "No, He is leading the people astray."

2. Jesus' brothers strangely offer him advice, expecting apparently that if he were in fact the Messiah, he would go to Jerusalem and show himself there to Israel in some auspicious way (Bernard, *Exegetical Commentary*, 1:266). This was because "it was widely believed that when the Messiah came he would make himself publicly known in some spectacular way. According to one rabbinic tradition, "He will come and stand on the roof of the holy place; and then he will announce to the Israelites, 'Ye poor, the time of your redemption has arrived'" (Bruce, *Gospel of John*, 170–71). Many Jews expected the coming Messiah to manifest himself at the Feast of Tabernacle (Ellis, *World of St. John*, 69). However, John has already mentioned that Jesus' brothers in fact do not actually believe in him (5:7). In any case, Jesus himself of course knew precisely the appropriate time and manner for his revelation to Israel and the world at large.

3. By "the world," Jesus here is referring to humanity in general. Recall John's testimony in the Prologue: "He was in the world, and the world was made through Him, but the world knew Him not" (1:10).

4. Jesus goes to Jerusalem in secret after telling his brothers "my time is not yet come," which reflects his intent not to court publicity as they have suggested (Bruce, *Gospel of John*, 173). The time for his public revelation to Israel as Messiah comes later (beginning in his extensive temple teaching, his entrance into Jerusalem on Palm Sunday and ultimately his crucifixion at Golgotha and resurrection from the garden tomb. From a narrative standpoint, John's Gospel 7:10 marks the end of Christ's Galilean ministry. John's focus shifts now to recording Jesus' extended teachings to the crowds, Pharisees, close friends (in Bethany), and his disciples in Jerusalem in the following period leading up to his passion, death, and resurrection.

13 No one was actually speaking openly about Him for fear of the Jews.

14 Already in the middle of the festival Jesus went up and was teaching in the temple.

15 Then the Jews were amazed saying, "How does He know learning without studying?"

16 Then Jesus answered them and said, "My teaching is not my own but that of the One who sent Me.

17 If anyone wishes to do His will, he will know concerning the teaching whether it is from God or whether I speak from Myself.

18 The one speaking from himself seeks his own glory; but the one seeking the glory of the One sending Him is true and there is no unrighteousness in Him.

19 Did not Moses give you the law; yet no one among you does the law. Why are you seeking to kill Me?"[5]

20 The crowd answered, "You have a demon; who seeks to kill you?"

21 Jesus answered and said to them, "I did one work, and all of you marvel.

22 On account of this Moses give you circumcision – not that of Moses but of the Fathers – and on the Sabbath you circumcise a man.

23 If a man receives circumcision on the Sabbath in order that the law of Moses might not be broken, and you are angry at Me because I made a whole man well on the Sabbath?

24 Do not judge by appearances but make a righteous judgment."[6]

---

5. During his last visit to Jerusalem, Jesus had invoked Moses as a witness against his accusers who sought the death sentence against him for healing the crippled man on the Sabbath. "Moses spoke of Him in advance as the coming prophet, yet [the Jewish religious authorities] gave no credence to Moses' testimony regarding Him" (see John 5:45–47). Now Jesus again invokes Moses against those attacking him. Here Jesus' point is that "for all their professed veneration of Moses' law, they themselves were guilty of breaking it" since Mosaic law dictated that "Thou shall not kill." Yet Jesus' persecutors were trying to have him put to death (Bruce, *Gospel of John*, 176).

6. The rite of circumcision was instituted in Abraham's time (Gen 17:10ff) and reiterated in the Mosaic law (Exod 12:44ff). "Jesus argues that if the sabbath law may be rightly suspended for the removal of a small piece of tissue from one part of the body, it cannot be wrong to heal a man's whole body on the sabbath day. This type of argument, in fact, was used by some rabbis to justify medical treatment in case of urgency on the sabbath, but Jesus uses it to justify an act of healing whether the case is urgent or not" (Bruce, *Gospel of John*, 177). Jesus' point is that healing done in God's name is as "holy" a Sabbath activity as circumcision. While the latter rite renders by physical marking the fact that a man has been set apart for God, the former action restores the body to the "whole", natural state of life as God intended it. Jesus' midrash of what the Torah recognizes as permitted sabbath activity includes both.

John Chapter 7

25 Then some of those living in Jerusalem were saying, "Is he not the one they are seeking to kill?

26 And behold, He speaks openly and they say nothing to him. Can it be that the authorities truly know that this is the Messiah?

27 But this one, we know where he is from; but when Messiah comes, no one will know where He is from."[7]

28 Then Jesus cried out in the Temple teaching and saying, "You know Me and You know where I am from; and I have not come from myself, but the One who sent me is true; Him you do not know.

29 I know Him, because I am from Him and He sent me."

30 Therefore they were seeking to arrest Him, but no one laid a hand on Him, because His hour had not yet come.[8]

31 But many from the crowd believed in Him and were saying, "When the Messiah comes, will He do more signs than this man did?"

32 The Pharisees heard the crowd murmuring these things about Him, and the chief priests and the Pharisees sent officers to arrest Him.

33 Then Jesus said, "Yet a little time I am with you and I am going to the One who sent Me.

34 You will seek Me and not find Me, and where I am you are not able to come."

35 Then the Jews said to one another, "How will he go where we cannot find him; is he about to go to the diaspora of the Greeks and to teach the Greeks?"

36 What is this word that He said, "You will seek me and not find and where I am you cannot come?"

37 And on the last day, the great day of the feast, Jesus stood up and cried out saying, "If anyone thirsts, let him come to Me and drink.

---

7. This is the first instance John records where the idea that Jesus is the Messiah being publicly debated in Jerusalem. The scene was a charged one, owing to traditional understanding of how the Messiah would appear. "It was widely believed that the Messiah after coming into the world would remain hidden until the appointed time for his public manifestation came. John ironically implies that those discussing Jesus' origins were thinking of His home in Galilee. To them he was [merely] 'Jesus of Nazareth'" (Bruce, *Gospel of John*, 178).

8. Cf. 7:8. Under God's providential direction, Jesus' enemies could not seize or harm him until the hour of his arrest, crucifixion, and death had come (ESV note).

The Gospel of John

38 The one believing in Me, as the Scripture says, streams of living water will flow from His heart."⁹

39 And He said this concerning the Spirit whom those believing in Him were about to receive. For the Spirit was not yet given, since Jesus had not yet been glorified. ¹⁰

40 Then those from the crowd hearing these words were saying, "He is truly the Prophet";¹¹

41 Others were saying, "He is the Messiah," but others were saying, "Does the Messiah come from Galilee?

42 Does not Scripture say that the Messiah comes from the seed of David and from Bethlehem, the village were David was?"¹²

---

9. *Sukkot,* Judaism's Feast of Ingathering, lasts eight days, and on the eighth day there is to be a holy convocation (Lev 23:36; Num 29:35ff; Neh 8:18). In the first century, when the people thanked God at this assembly for his gifts of the harvests of grapes, olives, barley and wheat, they included thanks for his gift of rain sufficient for the crops and necessary for their growth. A prayer for future rain for the coming year's crops was also recited on the eighth day (Bruce, *Gospel of John,* 181).

"The week of celebration [during *Sukkot*] was dominated by two Temple ceremonies, the water-pouring and the illumination of the Temple courts. Like the Passover, this festival also pointed to the future when healing water would flow from a renewed Temple (Ezekiel 47) and when 'night shall be no more' (Zech 14:7ff; Rev 22:5)" (Ellis, *World of St. John,* 69).

Commenting on the offering of water, Bernard quotes Rabbi Akiba: "'Bring the libation of the water at the Feast of Tabernacles, that the showers may be blessed to thee' . . a golden vessel was filled with water from the Pool of Siloam, and the water was solemnly offered by the priest, the singers chanting, 'With joy shall you draw water out of the wells of salvation' (Isa 12:3)" (Bernard, *Exegetical Commentary,* 1:281).

Jesus' offer here in 7:37–38 of his own, ever-sufficient, living-giving water on *Sukkot's* eighth day thus draws another link between his identity as Messiah and how, as Messiah, he stands *as the living embodiment and eternal fulfillment* of all the promises and prophesies of the Torah and the Prophets.

Importantly, the offer of living water had been made centuries before in the words of Isa 55:1: "Come! Everyone who thirsts, let him come to the waters . . ." Jesus in 7:37 repeats the offer declared in Isaiah, with a personal reference included: "If anyone is thirsty, let him come *to me*" (emph. added) (Bernard, *Exegetical Commentary,* 1:281).

10. Meaning the Holy Spirit was not yet present in the form that Jesus promised (Bruce, *Gospel of John,* 182–3). See John 20:22, Acts 2:1–13 ("we hear them telling in our own tongues the mighty works of God" (Acts 2:11b)). Of course, the presence of the Holy Spirit is hardly limited to the New Testament era. Deut 34:9, Micah 3:8, and numerous verses in Ezekiel and Daniel, as well as Gen 1:2 and 6:3 as a non-exhaustive list, make clear the presence and activity of God's Spirit on earth from the inception of creation.

11. Deut 18:15–19.

12. Micah 5:2 expressly declares that Bethlehem in Judea would be the birthplace of the "one who is to be the ruler of Israel." John and many of his readers know that

John Chapter 7

43 Therefore a schism arose in the crowd concerning Him.[13]
44 And some of them wanted to seize Him, but no one laid hands on Him.
45 Then the officers went to the chief priests and the Pharisees, and they said to them, "Why did you not bring him?"
46 The officers answered, "No one ever spoke like this man."
47 Then the Pharisees answered them, "Have you also have been deceived?
48 Did any of the chief priests or Pharisees believe in Him?
49 But this crowd not knowing the Law is accursed."
50 Nicodemus said to them, the one who had gone to Him previously,[14] being one of them,
51 "Does our law judge a man without first hearing from him and knowing what he does?"
52 They answered and said to him, "Are you also from Galilee? Search and see that no prophet arises out of Galilee."
53 And each one went to his own home.

Jesus was without question "born of the seed of David according to the flesh" (Rom 1:3) and that Judean Bethlehem, not Galilean Nazareth was his birthplace. The fallacy of the crowd's questioning of Jesus' status as Messiah based on an erroneous understanding of his incarnation at Bethlehem is a signal example of the narrative irony John employs at key moments in his gospel.

13. From this point on, the division arising in the crowd on Jesus' account becomes a recurring theme in John's account. But just as was the case earlier, an attempt to seize him comes to nothing. Jesus' time has "not yet come."

14. John 3:1–21.

8

John Chapter 8

VERSES 1-11[1]

1 And Jesus went to the Mount of Olives.
2 And again early in the morning he went to the Temple, and all the people came to Him, and sitting down He taught them.
3 And the Scribes and the Pharisees led a woman caught in adultery and putting her in their midst
4 They said to Him, "Teacher, this woman has been caught in the act of adultery.
5 Now in the law Moses commanded us to such kind of women. What then do you say?"

---

1. As Metzger notes, the manuscript evidence that the passage describing Jesus' encounter with the adulteress in 8:1–11 was not originally part of the Gospel of John is overwhelming; it is absent from a wide range of the earliest Greek manuscripts. The passage is also absent from the oldest and best forms of the Syriac version of the Gospel, and from various Coptic dialect versions. Moreover, no Greek Church Father comments on the passage until the twelfth century. In the West, the Gothic version and several Old Latin manuscripts omit it. This, together with the fact that (i) the style and vocabulary of this passage differ markedly from the rest of John's Gospel, and that (ii) it clearly interrupts what would otherwise a natural progression in the narrative from 7:52 to 8:12ff, strongly support the conclusion the passage is a later interpolation. At the same time, "the account has all the earmarks of historical veracity. It is obviously a piece of oral tradition which circulated in certain parts of the Western church and which was subsequently incorporated into various manuscripts at various places" (Metzger, *Textual Commentary*,187–89).

John Chapter 8

6 They were saying this to test Him, so that they might have grounds to accuse Him. But bending down Jesus wrote with His finger on the ground.
7 And when they kept asking Him, He stood up and said to them, "Let the one among you who is without sin be first to cast a stone upon her."
8 And bending down again, He wrote on the ground.
9 And those hearing went away one by one, beginning from the elders, and He alone remained standing with the woman before Him.
10 Standing up Jesus said to her, "Woman, where are they? Has no one condemned you?"
11 And she said, "No one, lord." And Jesus said to her, "Neither do I condemn you. Go, and from now sin no more."

* * *

REFLECTION: THE WOMAN IN THE CIRCLE

"... Cast the first stone."

Jesus' word of truth scatters the adulteress's would-be executioners. Indicted by their own hypocrisy, they leave the woman standing alone before Jesus.

However, she still remains under a death sentence, according to the Law (Deut 22:22).

In this moment, the same God who confronted the Hebrew people at Sinai in fire and thunder in effect says, "... to a self-confessed sinner with the guilt of the broken commandment heavy on her conscience, *neither do I condemn you.* Here is the miracle of the grace of God. There is no greater wonder than this."[2]

The righteous ones leave convicted, and the woman caught in the act of adultery leaves forgiven. Given the law's requirement, how is this possible? Only because Jesus is there. Jesus answers the adulteress—and all who humbly confess their sins—in the spirit of the higher law articulated in Hosea 6:6: "I desire mercy not sacrifice."

Remember: even though *we* bear the weight of sin and God's righteous judgment, *Jesus* answers the Law's requirement with the cross, once and for all. As with this woman, Christ is standing with us, patiently waiting, and asking:

"Where are they? Where are your would-be accusers?" (Satan, others, yourself?)

---

2. Milne, *Message of John*, 126.

"Does anyone condemn you? There is no one—they have gone. Neither do I condemn you. Go then and sin no more."

Thanks to Jesus' faithfulness for us unto death, nothing and no one stands or can stand between us and God. "Mercy triumphs over judgment" (James 2:13) only because of the cross. Jesus' tender mercy is good news to the adulteress, and to all us sinners, across the ages.

PRAYER

Lord, forgive me for all that I have done and left undone. The Law's requirements are clear, and I too stand in the circle of judgment. I understand your forgiveness is possible only because of Jesus' blessed sacrifice and victory over anything, any power, that would accuse or condemn. Thank you for faithfully standing with us in the circle, taking the penalty that is actually ours, and leading us out and leading us home. Thank you that your mercy is sufficient unto the day. Please remember me when your kingdom comes. Amen.

* * *

VERSES 12-59

12 Again then Jesus spoke to them saying, "I AM the light of the world. The one following me will not walk in darkness, but will have the light of life."[3]
13 Then the Pharisees said to Him, "You testify concerning yourself; your testimony is not true."[4]
14 Jesus answered and said to them, "Even if I testify concerning Myself, My testimony is true, because I know whence I came and where I am going. But you do not know where I come from or where I am going.

---

3. Jesus as the servant of the Lord and the Word incarnate embodies the Old Testament language of God as his people's light (Ps 27:1). In the light of his presence, they enjoy grace and peace (Num 6:24–26). The servant of the Lord shines as a light to the nations, that God's salvation may extend to the end of the earth (Isa 49:6). Similarly, the word or law of God is also a light to guide the path of the obedient (Ps 119:105; Prov 6:23) (Bruce, *Gospel of John*, 188).

4. Mosaic law (Deut 19:15) requires the testimony of more than one witness to convict for a crime. Jesus himself, when confronted by Jewish leaders over "Sabbath-breaking" when healing the invalid at the Pool of Bethesda in chapter 5 makes clear that "If I alone bear witness about myself, my witness is not true" (5:31). The Lord went on to explain at that point that he in fact has another witness concerning himself: John the Baptist is 'the other' who bears witness about him "and I know that the testimony that he bears about me is true" (5:32). The Pharisees here continue the same dispute (NIV).

John Chapter 8

15 You judge according to the flesh, I judge no one.[5]

16 And if I do judge, my judgment is true, because I am not alone, but I and the One sending me the Father.

17 And in your Law it is written that the testimony of two people is true.

18 *I AM* the One witnessing concerning myself, and the Father the One sending me witnesses concerning Me."[6]

19 They then said to Him, "Where is your father?" Jesus answered, "You neither know Me, nor My Father. If you had known Me, you would have also known My Father."

20 He spoke these words in the treasury, teaching in the Temple;[7] but no one seized Him, because His hour had not yet come.

21 Again He said to them, "I am going and you [pl.] will seek Me, and you will die in your sin. Where I am going you cannot come."

22 Then the Jews were saying, "Will he kill himself, since he says, 'Where I am going you cannot come?'"

23 And He said to them, "You are from below, I am from above; you are from this world, I am not from this world.

24 Therefore I said to you that you will die in your sins; for unless you believe that I AM, you will die in your sins."[8]

25 Then they said to Him, "Who are you?" Jesus said to them, "That which from the beginning I have been saying to you.

---

5. Jesus is indeed the One to whom God has given all judgment (5:22), even if at this juncture he does not exercise this prerogative. In his incarnation Christ came to bring salvation, not to pronounce judgment (Bruce, *Gospel of John*, 189). The Pharisees are judging "according to the flesh" because they either do not understand or refuse to recognize Jesus is in God the Father and the Father is in Him (14:11). Thus they misjudge his testimony as inadequate because they fail to see God's inherent support of all of Jesus' messianic claims, as Jesus points in v. 17–18.

6. Jesus here introduces God the Father, "the One who sent me" as his witness (in addition to John the Baptist).

7. There were offering collection chests against one wall in the court of women, a forecourt of the temple (Coffman, "Commentaries," verse 20). It was a very public place, at the center of temple religious life, where Jesus taught. The Sanhedrin met "within earshot" of this place, explaining its proximity (both locationally and in the Gospel's narrative) of the adulteress brought before Jesus before her 'sentence' was to be executed.

8. Jesus quotes God's personal name—the Tetragrammaton YHWH that God uses in self-revelation to Moses before the Burning Bush in Exod 3:14—as he points out the Jewish leaders' state of spiritual death, their unbelief in him and his revelation as God.

26 I have many things concerning you to say and to judge, but the One who sent Me is true, and I declare to the world the things which I heard from Him."

27 They did not know that He was speaking to them of the Father.

28 Then Jesus said to them, "When you have lifted up the Son of Man, then you will know that 'I AM,' and that I do nothing from Myself, but just as the Father taught Me these things I say.

29 And the One who sent me is with Me; He has not left me alone, for I always do what is pleasing to Him."

30 As He was speaking these things many believed in Him.[9]

31 Then Jesus said to the Jews who believed in Him, "If you remain in My word, you are truly My disciples,[10]

32 and you will know the truth, and the truth will set you free."

33 They answered Him, "We are the seed of Abraham, and have never been slaves, how are you saying that, 'You will become free?'"

34 Jesus answered them, "Truly, truly I say to you that everyone who sins is a servant of sin.

35 And the servant does not remain in the house forever, the Son remains forever.

36 Therefore if the Son sets you free, you will be free indeed.[11]

---

9. Note the contrast between the Jewish leaders' unbelief and "the many" in the crowd who believed in Jesus after hearing his teaching.

10. The apparent anomaly between John's reference in v. 30–31 to "believers" and Jesus' stated view that these people are actually slaves to sin (8:31), indifferent to his word (8:37), children of the devil (8:44), and liars (8:55) can be explained as either (1) another example of fickle or superficial faith, a theme that John registered earlier (see 6:60, 64–65) (Carson's note on 'the children of Abraham' in 8:31–59), or (2) a reflection of the fact that at some point early in this polemical exchange "the circle of [Jesus'] interlocutors widens; by the time v. 37 is reached, it is unbelieving Jews who are addressed" (Bruce, *Gospel of John*, 197). The fact that Jesus goes on to set out in this verse what separates superficial from true faith—'abiding/remaining in' his word—gives the first reading greater weight.

11. The freedom Jesus brings is deliverance from enslavement to sin (recall 1:17: "the law came through Moses, but grace and truth came through Jesus Christ").

Jesus uses the parenthetical parable of the servant and the son here to affirm that he alone is the agent of such freedom (Rom 8:2 "For the law of the Spirit of life has seen you free in Christ Jesus from the law of sin and death") (Bernard, *Exegetical Commentary*, 2:305; Robertson, *Word Pictures*, 5:150–51). The underlying argument of his teaching could be summarized as follows: by definition, a servant has no permanent standing in his master's house. In contrast, the son in a free household who comes of age can act with authority precisely because of his status as a son. Likewise, Jesus as God's Son acts with supreme authority because "the Father loves the Son and has given all things into His hand" (3:35). As God's only begotten Son, Christ is the sole agent of emancipation

37 I know that you are the seed of Abraham; yet you seek to kill Me, because My word has no place[12] in you.

38 I speak of that which I have seen with the Father; you also do what you heard from the father."[13]

39 They answered and said to Him, "Our father is Abraham." Jesus said to them, "If you are children of Abraham, you would be doing the works of Abraham;

40 But now you seek to kill me, a man who has spoken to you the truth which I heard from God; this Abraham did not do.[14]

41 You are doing the works of your father." They said to Him, "We have not been born from sin; we have one father, God."[15]

42 Jesus said to them, "If God was your father you would love Me, for I came forth from God and am here; for I have not come of Myself, but He sent Me.

43 Why do you not understand what I say? It is because you are not able to hear My word.

44 You are from your father the devil and you wish to do the desires of your father. He was a murderer from the beginning, and was not standing in the truth, because truth is not in him. When he speaks lies, he speaks from himself, because he is a liar and the father of lies.

45 And because I speak the truth, you do not believe Me.

46 Which of you convicts me of sin? If I speak the truth, why do you not believe me?

---

from slavery to sin (Bernard, *Exegetical Commentary*, 2:208). Therefore, if based on the authority given to him by the Father, Jesus frees a slave, the slave is free indeed (Bruce, *Gospel of John*, 197–98).

12. The literal sense of the Greek verb *koreo* (χωρέω) here is "to find room, make progress." Jesus is saying that his word finds no room in the hearts and minds of those purportedly believing in him (8:30–31).

13. For Jesus' meaning here, see v. 44.

14. Abraham welcomed heavenly messengers in Gen 18:3. Those opposing Jesus display a very different kind of conduct, belying a very different kind of 'father' (Bruce, *Gospel of John*, 199; Bernard, *Exegetical Commentary*, 2:311).

15. Responding to Jesus' statement in v. 24 that the Pharisees and others disputing his Messiahship would die in their sins unless they believed in him. Those opposing Jesus believe their spiritual sonship in Abraham is sufficient, notwithstanding that Messiah has come. "People who need to be set free are bound or enslaved, but those speaking with Jesus tragically have no consciousness of bondage . . . The promise to Abraham spoke of blessing for his descendants, and freedom was an essential element in that blessing" (Bruce, *Gospel of John*, 197).

The Gospel of John

47 Whoever is of God hears the words of God; because of this you do not hear, because you are not of God."

48 The Jews answered and said to Him, "Do we not speak rightly in saying that you are a Samaritan and you have a demon?"
49 Jesus answered, "I do not have a demon, but I honor My Father, and you dishonor Me.
50 And I do not seek My own glory; there is One who seeks and judges.[16]
51 Truly, truly I say to you, if anyone keeps My word, he will never see death."[17]
52 Then the Jews said to Him, "Now we know that you have a demon. Abraham and the prophets died, and you say, 'If anyone keeps My word, he will never taste death.'
53 Are you greater than our father Abraham, who died? And the prophets died. Who do you make yourself?"
54 Jesus answered, "If I glorify Myself, My Gory is nothing. It is My Father who glorifies Me, the One whom you say 'He is our God,'
55 You have not known Him, but I know Him, and if I should say that I do not know Him, I will be a liar like you; but I know Him and I keep His word.
56 Your father Abraham rejoiced that he beheld my day, and he saw and was glad."
57 Then the Jews said to Him, "You are not yet fifty years old and you have seen Abraham?"
58 Jesus said to them, "Truly, truly I say to you, before Abraham was born, I AM."
59 Then they took up stones in order to stone Him. But Jesus hid Himself and went out from the Temple.

---

16. Jesus is content as long as he has the Father's approval. He is not concerned for his own reputation (Bruce, *Gospel of John*, 203). Would that I had more of the strong, trusting faith that Jesus models here!

17. "See" in the Greek here (*theoreo*, θεωρέω) carries the meaning of "undergo" or "experience." In other words, as Bruce notes, "the message that Jesus brings delivers those who hear and keep it from eternal death" (Bruce, *Gospel of John*, 203). Jesus doesn't promise that believers are somehow spared from physical death. His point is rather that "the property of death is so altered that [faithful believers] do not see . . . the terror of death . . . They shall not see death *forever*. The day will come when *death shall be swallowed up in victory* . . . They shall have their everlasting lot where there will be *no more death*, where they *cannot die any longer*" (Henry, *Henry's Commentary*, 1555).

9

John Chapter 9

VERSES 1-5

1 And passing by, He saw a man blind from birth.
2 And the disciples asked Him about him saying, "Rabbi, who sinned, this man or his parents, that he was born blind?"[1]
3 Jesus answered, "Neither he sinned nor his parents, but that the works of God might be revealed in him.
4 It is necessary for us to do the work of the One who sent Me while it is day; night is coming when no one will be able to work.
5 While I am in the world, I am light of the world."

*   *   *

REFLECTION: I AM THE LIGHT OF THE WORLD

In this the second of His seven "I AM" statements in John's gospel, before he heals the blind man, Jesus declares Himself "the light of the world."

To understand Jesus' miracle here, the sixth such "sign" recounted by John, recall John 1:4, which teaches that in Jesus is light, and that this light is the light of all humanity. Also 1:3, which affirms also that through Jesus all things

---

1. The text doesn't indicate how the disciples know that the man is born blind. Their question however reflects the same mistaken assumption about divine retribution that Job's friends make in the process of trying to comfort him in his afflictions in Scripture's longest meditation on theodicy and its challenges, the book of Job.

were created, and without him nothing was made that was made. Jesus' light brings life.

Commenting on this passage, fourth-century Church Father Ephrem the Syrian wrote that Jesus with his "anointing of mud" on the man in effect re-enacts God's work of creation in Genesis (2:7—"then the Lord God formed the man of dust from the ground and breathed into his nostrils the breath of life, and the man became a living creature.") As God did at the beginning, Jesus does in this man's life. He brings forth "the light from the dust." As Jesus forms clay with his saliva and then anoints the man's eyes with it, he "supplied what was lacking in creation" (sight for this man blind from birth), "to show that what was lacking in nature was being supplied by his hand" (ACCS, Ephrem comment on John 9:5).

PRAYER

Consider the power of Jesus' light-giving life and his gift of literal illumination to the man born blind. Are there areas of blindness in your life that need Christ's light? How might God desire to reveal his work in you today? Ask God to enlighten your mind and spirit, and show you the work he has for you to do.

Father, shine your light to give our darkened minds true knowledge of you. Fill our hearts with the perseverance and mercy of your blessed spirit, that we might see as Jesus sees, and do as he says, to help and serve others. In your mercy, please hear this prayer. Amen!

*   *   *

VERSES 6–41

6 Saying these things, He spit on the ground and made mud with His spit and smeared the mud on his eyes[2]
7 and said to him, "Go wash in the Pool of Siloam (which means 'Sent')."[3] Then he went and washed and came back seeing.

---

2. To my knowledge, anointings with mud unto healing are not otherwise attested in Scripture. Such is the power of Christ's transforming touch that even mud formed by him works healing.

3. What's in a name? The Greek name Siloam in the Hebrew is *shiloah* (שִׁלֹחַ). Isaiah records the Lord's lament that Israel has "refused the gently flowing waters of Shiloah," resulting in judgment at the hand of the king of Assyria, "the river with mighty and many waters" (Isa 8:6). The name derives from the Hebrew word *shalach* (שלח), to send, and clearly refers to Jesus, the one sent of God "who alone is qualified to impart inward

John Chapter 9

8 Then the neighbors and those who had seen him before as a beggar were saying; "Is not this not the one used to sit and beg?"
9 Some were saying that it is he, others were saying no, but it is one who looks like him. He kept saying "I am the man."[4]
10 So they said to him, "How then were your eyes opened?"
11 He answered, "The man called Jesus made mud and spread it on my eyes and said to me 'Go to the Siloam and wash'; then I went and washed, and received sight."
12 And they said to him, "Where is he?" He said, "I do not know."
13 They took to the Pharisees the man who had formerly been blind.
14 And it was the Sabbath on the day when Jesus made the mud and opened his eyes.
15 Again the Pharisees were asking him, how did he receive sight. And he said to them, "He put mud on my eyes, and I washed and I see."
16 Then some of the Pharisees were saying, "This man is not from God, because he does not keep the Sabbath." Others were saying, "How could a sinful man do such signs?" So there was a schism among them.
17 Then they said to the blind man again, "What do you say concerning him, since he opened your eyes?" And he said, "He is a prophet."[5]

---

illumination" (Bruce, *Gospel of John*, 210).

Against this background, consider how, in the act of healing the man, Jesus first sends him to wash in the pool of Siloam in the City of David which was fed by water from the spring of Gihon in the Kidron Valley, then to the Pharisees and to the blind man's own family and community, and finally figuratively into centuries of history since, as a witness to Jesus' power to heal not only physical but spiritual blindness. Having been made well and given his testimony to the Pharisees ("if this man were not from God, he could do nothing"; 8:33), the man later "sees" Jesus not only as his healer but also as his Lord, worthy of worship ("'Lord, I believe'"; 8:38).

As the beloved hymn Amazing Grace tells, ". . . I once was lost, but now am found, 'twas blind but now I see."

4. Fascinatingly, the former cripple quotes Christ's own words of power I AM (ἐγώ εἰμι) as he self-identifies as indeed the one healed by the one identifying himself in very nature God.

5. Augustine in his commentary on this passage notes that the formerly blind man ". . . declares openly what he thinks. For he said, "He is a prophet." Not yet anointed in heart, he could not confess [Jesus as being] the Son of God. Nevertheless, he is not wrong in what he says either, for our Lord even says of himself, "A prophet is not without honor except in his own country." Jesus is "the personification of Siloam" for Augustine (Tractates on the Gospel of John 44.9 [ACCS]).

18 But the Jews were not believing concerning him, that he was blind and received sight, until they called the parents of the man who had received his sight

19 and asked them saying, "This is your son, whom you say was born blind. How then does he now see?"

20 Then his parents answered and said, "We know that he is our son and that he was born blind;

21 But how now he sees we do not know, nor do we know who opened his eyes; ask him, he is of age, he will speak for himself."

22 His parents said these things because they feared the Jews; for the Jews had already agreed that if anyone confessing him as Christ would be cast out from the community of the synagogue.

23 Because of this his parents said that, "He is of age, ask him."

24 Therefore they called the man a second time, the one who had been blind and said to him, "Give glory to God; we know that this man is a sinner."

25 He answered, "I do not know if he is a sinner; one thing I do know is that being blind now I see."[6]

26 Then they said to him, "What did he do for you? How did he open your eyes?"

27 He answered them, "I told you already and you did not hear? Why do you wish to hear again? Do you wish to become His disciples?"

28 And they reviled him and said, "You are his disciple, but we are disciples of Moses.

29 We know that God has spoken through Moses, but we do not know where this man comes from."

30 The man answered and said to them, "This is amazing indeed, that you do not know where He is from, and He opened my eyes.[7]

31 For we know that God does not hear sinners, but if anyone is God-fearing and does His will, him He hears.

---

6. The formerly blind man continues his journey to faith. His responses to the Jewish leaders in the passage show a growing awareness as God's mercy keeps working to open his spiritual eyes, even as Jesus has already graciously healed his physical eyes. In contrast, the synagogue leaders while having physical sight remain spiritually blind, unable to see Jesus as the incarnated Messiah and the great I AM.

7. The narrative irony here is palpable as the healed man rejoins the Jewish leaders' attack upon him by asking if they wish to become Jesus' disciple, and then expresses amazement at the Jewish leaders' own spiritual blindness in failing to recognize Christ's healing work over his eyes as a miracle of God.

John Chapter 9

32 Since the beginning of the world it has never been heard that anyone opened the eyes of a person born blind;

33 If this man were not from God, He would not be able to do anything."

34 They answered and said to him, "You were wholly born in sin and you teach us?"[8] And they cast him out.

35 Jesus heard that they had cast him out and finding him said, "Do you believe in the Son of Man?"

36 He answered and said, "And who is it, lord, that I may believe in him"?

37 Jesus said to him, "Indeed you have seen Him, and the One speaking with you is He."

38 And he said, "Lord, I believe"; and he fell down to worship Him.[9]

39 And Jesus said, "For judgment I came into this world, so that those not seeing would see, and those seeing would become blind."

40 Those with Him from the Pharisees heard these things and said to Him, "Are we also blind?"

41 Jesus said to them, "If you were blind, you would not have sin; but now that you say that 'we see,' your sin remains."

---

8. The Pharisees' angry response shows that they realize they are losing the argument. Based on their own principles there was no answering the healed man's logic. The reference to "wholly born in sin" implies that (like Jesus' disciples) the Pharisees believe the man's former blindness was due to either his parents' sin or his own (Bruce, *Gospel of John*, 219).

9. Notice that Jesus asks the one remaining necessary question of the man now healed: "Do you believe in the Son of Man?" Jesus' healing of the blind man is a "parable of spiritual illumination." With the Advent of Jesus' Light of the World, those in darkness (whether by sin or a physical handicap) are helped to see. At the same time, those supposedly able to see but who reject Jesus move into deeper darkness. Had the Pharisees acknowledged their own spiritual blindness and sin and allowed Christ to heal it, they too would have been blessed. As it was, as Jesus maintains their sin remains (Bruce, *Gospel of John*, 220–21).

10

John Chapter 10

VERSES 1-10

1 "Truly, truly I say to you, the one who does not enter through the gate of the sheepfold but climbs up some other way, that one is a thief and a robber;
2 But the One entering by the gate is shepherd of the sheep.[1]
3 The gatekeeper opens to Him, and the sheep listen to His voice, and He calls His sheep by name and leads them out.
4 When He has brought out all His own, He goes before them, and the sheep follow Him, because they know His voice;
5 But they will not follow a stranger, but will flee from him, because they do not know the voice of the stranger."
6 Jesus spoke this parable to them, but they did not understand what he was saying to them.

7 Then Jesus again said, "Truly, truly I say to you that I am the gate for the sheep.

---

1. Here and in the following verses we encounter the theme of God as shepherd to his people Israel. Together with that of the Messiah as shepherd, this image would have been a familiar one to Jesus' listeners, given the pastoral setting of their time. See Ezek 34 for God's declaration that because of selfish and immoral shepherds who were feeding *on* rather than feeding and caring *for* the flock, God himself would shepherd, seek the lost, and feed his people "in justice." Micah 5:4 and Isa 40:11 are examples of Hebrew scriptures' image of the messianic king as tending the flock of YHWH (Bernard, *Exegetical Commentary*, 2:345).

8 All who came before Me are thieves and robbers, but the sheep did not listen to them.

9 I am the gate; if anyone enters through Me he will be saved, and will enter in and will go out and will find pasture.

10 The thief comes not but to steal and murder and destroy; I came that they might have life and have it abundantly."

*   *   *

REFLECTION: THE ABUNDANT LIFE

Is there enough?

I find it ironic, notwithstanding the manifold mercies and opportunities that so many of us enjoy, particularly those living in so-called "first world" countries, how prone we are to view life and our position in the world today in terms of scarcity.

In one sense a preoccupation with scarcity is not a surprising, or indeed an ill-founded view: growing scarcity of natural resources, food, water and energy are already without question acute global problems, especially in lesser-developed nations. If not addressed these challenges will be present crises for tomorrow's generation.

So perhaps the true irony lies in how we often extend this mindset of inherent scarcity from the material world to *spiritual* matters. Speaking personally, I know that the technology-enabled "convenience" of the twenty-first century can breed within me a limited view of God that often defaults to doubt and complaint whenever I face pain, fear, or uncertainty, whether from a cancer scan result, personal conflict, or some other unpleasant situation. When the ground below me unexpectedly shifts and that big problem emerges, my first impulse all too often is not to acknowledge my need and trustfully seek the Lord's mercy and provision. Rather, I confront God and ask, Lord, have you got this? Where are you in this moment, this "in the meantime" time of uncomfortable unknowing? I can't believe how *inconvenient* this is. Do you care?

Of course we should be honest with God, including with our deepest doubts and fears. Jesus certainly was, as we know from his prayers in Gethsamane (Matt 26:39, 42; Mark 14:36, 39; Luke: 22:42, 44) and his anguished cry from the cross recorded in Matt 27:46 and Mark 15:34 (quoting Ps 22:1).

But as Jesus' words in John 10:10 attest, the spiritual side of life—unlike how spiritual matters can often be—is not a zero-sum game. Christ is the author and provider of true abundance. By my count Jesus never ran out of anything during his earthly ministry. Most importantly, he never exhausted his divine reservoir of power to bless, heal, and deliver.

So the question is not whether the God I worship is big enough. The question is can I look beyond *my* limitations and circumstances to see him, for all that he is and desires to be for those who know and follow him. From this perspective, we experience life's rich, inner fullness most vividly when we trust God for all the big things and walk with him daily in childlike trust. Can you and I accept this often non-intuitive truth? Real joy is the conviction that he truly is all that he says he is, and based on that belief, to trust and love him with some measure of how he first loved us.

"... I came that they might have life, and have it abundantly."

PRAYER

Lord, the Bible says that you desire truth within (Ps 51:6). Please impart your truth to our hearts so that we don't miss where true abundance lies. Only in the life hidden with you, in Christ, can our be hearts full and fully at peace. Please grant us this abundant life. In your holy name, Amen.

* * *

VERSES 11-42

11 "I AM the good shepherd. The good shepherd lays down his life for the sheep;

12 The hired hand indeed not being a shepherd—the sheep are not his own—sees the wolf coming and abandons the sheep and flees—and the wolf seizes and scatters them—

13 Because a hired hand indeed cares not for the sheep.

14 I AM the good shepherd and I know those who are mine and they know Me, [2]

15 Just as the Father knows Me and I know the Father, and I lay down My life for the sheep.[3]

---

2. Jesus affirms that he knows every sheep in his flock. Including you and I. The good shepherd knows us! Jesus brings life; false shepherds bring death (Guthrie, *New Bible Commentary*, 951).

3. The mark of the true shepherd is to know his sheep, recalling Num 16:5: "The Lord knows who are His" (Septuagint; see Bruce, *Gospel of John*, 227). Notice also how the intimacy of the Shepherd with His sheep depends and is grounded on the intimacy of the Father and the Son (NICNT).

John Chapter 10

16 And I have other sheep that are not of this fold.[4] I must bring [them] also, and they will listen to My voice, and so there will be one flock, one shepherd.

17 Because of this the Father loves me, because I lay down My life, so that again I may take it up.[5]

18 No one takes it from Me, but I give it from Myself. I have authority to lay it down, and I have authority again to take it up. This commandment I received from My Father."

19 Again a schism arose amongst the Jews because of these words.[6]

20 And many of them were saying, "He has a demon and is insane; why do you listen to him?"

21 Others were saying, "These are not the words of a demon-possessed person. Can a demon open the eyes of one born blind?"[7]

22 And at that time it was the Feast of Dedication[8] in Jerusalem. It was winter,

23 And Jesus was walking in the Temple, in the Portico of Solomon.

24 Then the Jews surrounded Him and were saying to Him, "How long will you keep us in suspense? If you are the Christ, speak to us plainly."[9]

25 Jesus answered them, "I spoke to you and you do not believe. The works that I do in the Name of My Father, these testify concerning Me;

26 But you do not believe, because you are not from my sheep.

27 My sheep listen to My voice and I know them and they follow Me,

28 And I give them eternal life and they will never perish and no one will snatch them out of My hand.

---

4. That is, the gentiles.

5. In other words, God's love for Jesus is "drawn out" by the Lord's willing sacrifice of his life, so that he can then resume it after his resurrection, for the good of humanity (Bernard, *Exegetical Commentary*, 2:364). Only by dying and falling to the ground could the grain of wheat "bear much fruit" (John 12:24) (Bruce, *Gospel of John*, 228).

6. Jesus' hearers now take sides, for or against Him.

7. Jesus' supporters point out that his healing power does not and cannot come from a demon. As Jesus himself testified in 10:10 Satan comes only to kill and destroy, Christ comes that his sheep may have life and have it abundantly.

8. That is, Hanukkah.

9. The temple authorities continued to seek evidence for a charge of blasphemy that they could bring against Jesus. According to Mosaic law, blasphemy was punishable by death (Lev 24:16).

The Gospel of John

29 My Father who has given [them] to Me is greater than all, and no one can snatch [them] from the hand of the Father.[10]

30 I and the Father are one."[11]

31 The Jews took up stones again to stone Him.

32 Jesus answered them, "I showed you many good works from the Father. For which of these works are you stoning me?"

33 The Jews answered Him, "We are not stoning you for good works but for blasphemy, and because you being a man are making yourself God."[12]

34 Jesus answered them, "Is it not written in your law that 'I said, you are gods?'[13]

35 If He called them gods to whom the Word of God came, and Scripture cannot be broken,

36 He whom the Father consecrated and sent into the world, you say that 'You are blaspheming,' because I said, 'I am the Son of God'?

37 If I am not doing the works of My Father, then do not believe Me.

38 But if I do [do these works], and you do not believe Me, believe in the works, so that you may know and understand that the Father [is] in Me and I [am] in the Father."

39 Then again they sought to seize Him, but He escaped from their hands.

40 And He went away again across the Jordan to the place where John was first baptizing, and stayed there.

---

10. Note the contrast with the case of the hired hand in vv. 12–13, who abandons the sheep in time of danger (ESV study note). Those whom Jesus protects, God protects. The ones whom Jesus keeps in his hand, God keeps in his (Bruce, *Gospel of John*, 232). This is the promise of Ps 73:23–24: "Yet I am always with You; You hold my right hand. By Your counsel you will guide and afterwards You will receive me in glory." We have the promise of God's grace, sealed with the blessing of Christ's might hand ever holding us close.

11. Jesus' "shattering statement" answers, if indirectly, all the temple authorities' prior questions: "from where is your father, who are you, tell us plainly if you are the Christ," etc. (Bruce, *Gospel of John*, 232). With his self-identification with the Father Jesus leaves no doubt as to his divinity and nature.

12. Sadly, the Jewish authorities and those incited by them in the temple can neither accept nor believe Jesus' claims regarding his identity.

13. The scriptural reference Jesus quotes here is Ps 82:6. Psalm 82 admonishes human rulers of God's people, who are called "gods" by virtue of their appointment, to act justly. In John 10:35, Jesus draws an ironic contrast between the former prophets or judges "to whom the word of God came" (the only time Christ uses this phrase in John's Gospel [NICNT]), and himself, God's very own "word," embodied in human form. Jesus' point is that if Scripture calls human leaders to whom God's Word came "gods," how possibly could Jesus be "blaspheming" with his implicit claim of Sonship by his references to "My Father"?

John Chapter 10

41 And many went to Him and were saying that while John did no sign, everything John said about Him was true.

42 And many there believed in Him.

11

John Chapter 11

VERSES 1-16

1 Now a certain man was ill, Lazarus from Bethany, of the village of Mary and Martha her sister.
2 And it was Mary, the one who anointed the Lord with myrrh and wiped His feet with her hair, whose brother Lazarus was ill.
3 Then the sisters sent to Him saying, "Lord, behold, the one whom you love is sick."
4 When Jesus heard this He said, "This sickness is not unto death but for the glory of God, so that the Son of God might be glorified through it."[1]
5 Now Jesus loved Martha and her sister and Lazarus.
6 When He then heard that he [Lazarus] was ill, He still stayed in the place where He was for two days,
7 Then after this He said to the disciples, "let us go again into Judea."
8 The disciples said to Him, "Rabbi, just now the Jews were seeking to stone you, and you are going there again?"[2]

---

1. This is the first time in John's Gospel that Jesus mentions his glorification, promising that he will somehow be glorified through Lazarus's sickness. The sisters surely could not have understood Jesus' words before they saw their brother raised (NICNT). The story of Lazarus's death and resurrection anticipates Christ's later glorification of God through his own death on the cross and resurrection.

2. The disciples correctly recognize the potential danger in returning to Jerusalem and its nearby regions. The village of Bethany where Lazarus and his sisters lived was only several miles east of Jerusalem.

9 Jesus answered, "Are there not twelve hours in the day? If anyone should walk in the day, he does not stumble, because he sees the light of this world;
10 But if someone should walk at night, he stumbles, because the light is not in him."
11 He said these things, and after this He said to them, "Our friend Lazarus sleeps; but I go to awaken him."
12 Then the disciples said to Him, "Lord, if he sleeps, he will be saved."[3]
13 But Jesus had spoken of his death, but they thought that he had spoken of taking rest in sleep.
14 So then Jesus told them plainly, "Lazarus has died,
15 And I am glad for your sake that I was not there, so that you may believe. But let us go to him."
16 Then Thomas the one called Didymos said to his fellow disciples, "Let us go also, that we may die with him."[4]

* * *

REFLECTION: THOMAS' ASIDE

"Let us go also, that we may die with him."

Thomas clearly does not believe Jesus' statement in 11:4 that Lazarus's sickness is not "unto death but for the glory of God." What are the chances that you or I would say the same thing or something similar to Thomas's almost humorous mutter, if we were in his position? It is a wonder of Jesus' mercy that notwithstanding our own skepticism, doubts and fears, he continues to lead and teach us with grace and love today, just as he did for Thomas two thousand years ago.

* * *

3. The disciples' natural interpretation of Jesus' statement was that Lazarus being ill had fallen into what would be a refreshing or healing slumber (Bernard, *Exegetical Commentary*, 2:364).

4. While sounding almost humorously ironic to our hears, Thomas's voice is in fact one of unbelief and fear. Seemingly included (by implication) in the resigned skepticism that Thomas voices, the disciples as a group recede entirely from view in the rest of the Lazarus pericope and don't reappear in the narrative until Jesus withdraws to Ephraim (11:54) after increased opposition from the temple authorities having received word of Jesus' raising of Lazarus (NICNT).

VERSES 17-44

17 Coming then Jesus found him having already been in the tomb for four days.
18 And Bethany was near Jerusalem, about fifteen stadia off.[5]
19 And many of the Jews had come to Martha and Mary to comfort them concerning their brother.
20 Then Martha when she heard that Jesus comes met Him; but Mary was sitting at home.[6]
21 Then Martha said to Jesus, "LORD, if You were here, my brother would not have died.[7]
22 [But] even now I know that whatever You may ask of God, God will give to you."[8]
23 Jesus said to her, "Your brother will rise again."[9]
24 Martha said to Him, "I know that he will rise again in the resurrection on the last day."[10]
25 Jesus said to her, "I AM the resurrection and the life; the one believing in me, even if he should die, yet will he live.
26 And that everyone who lives and believes in me will never die. Do you believe this?"
27 She said to Him, "Yes LORD, I have believed that You are the Christ, the Son of God, the One coming into the world."[11]

---

5. In modern units of measurement, slightly under two miles.

6. The sense of the Greek is that "as soon as Martha heard Jesus had come she met him." Apparently somehow the news had not yet reached Mary (see the parallel verse recording Mary's going to meet Him in v. 29).

7. Note that no words of greeting are recounted by John; in the narrative "silence" we sense the frustration and pain (pain?) that Martha's words carry, even if she doesn't consciously intend this as a rebuke (v. 22 indeed affirms her continuing faith in Jesus and the power of His prayer to the Father). Nevertheless her statement could be read with the connotation of "Lord, why did You let my brother die?"

8. As is often the case amongst all church fathers, Augustine's observation is most apt—Martha simply trusts that Jesus knows what is best: "She does not say to Him, 'Bring my brother to life again.' For how could she know that it would be good for him to come to life again? She says [in effect] I know that You can do so, if You want to, but what You will do is for your judgment, not for presumption, to determine" (ACCS).

9. Words of love, words of power!

10. Martha follows the view of the Pharisees (Acts 23:8), most first-century Jews and Jesus' teaching (John 5:21, 25-29; 6:39-44, 54) regarding the eschatological day of resurrection for the righteous (ESV note on 11:24).

11. Jesus Christ the Lord is God's dayspring from on high (ἀνατολὴ ἐξ ὕψους; Luke

John Chapter 11

28 And when she had said this she went and called Mary her sister in private saying, "The Teacher has come and is calling for you."

29 And when she [Mary] heard she arose at once and went to Him.

30 And Jesus had not yet come to the village but was still in the place where Martha met Him.

31 Then the Jews who were with her in the house and comforting her saw Mary that she arose quickly and went out, followed her, supposing that she was going to the tomb to weep there.

32 So Mary when she came to the place where Jesus was and seeing Him fell at His feet, saying to Him, "Lord, if You were here my brother would not have died."[12]

33 Then when He saw her weeping and the Jews who had come with her weeping, Jesus was greatly moved in spirit and was troubled Himself,[13]

34 And He said, "Where you have laid him?" They said to Him, "Lord, come and see."

35 Jesus wept.[14]

36 Then the Jews said, "Behold how he loved him!"

37 But some of them said, "Was not he who opened the eyes of the blind man able to cause this man not to die?"

38 Jesus again greatly moved within Himself came to the tomb; and there was a cave and a stone was laying against it.

39 Jesus said, "Take away the stone." Martha the sister of the dead man said to Him, "Lord, there is already a smell, for it is four days."

40 Jesus said to her, "Did I not say to you that if you believe you will see the glory of God?"

41 So they took away the stone. And Jesus lifted up His eyes and said, "Father, I thank You, because You heard me.

42 I knew that You always hear me, but because of the crowd standing [here] I spoke, so that they might believe that You sent Me."

43 And saying these things, with a loud voice He cried out, "Lazarus, come out!"

1:78), coming into the world to save and conquer sin, death, and evil within it.

12. Notice how Mary here repeats Martha's words recorded in 11:21.

13. Jesus is ever compassionate to those who are grieving so! Christ understands and experiences our suffering with us. Any suggestion of Jesus' anger by certain commentators' construction of the verbs here is best understood as his anger at the injustice of death and the pain it causes to the living.

14. One of Scripture's most profound verses.

44 The dead man came out, feet and hands bound with strips of cloth and his face wrapped with a cloth. Jesus said to them, "Unbind him and let him go."[15]

* * *

REFLECTION: "LAZARUS, COME OUT!"

Jesus' raising of Lazarus is the last and greatest of His seven "miraculous signs." To review, Jesus' previous six miracles recorded in John's gospel are:

- turning water into wine at the wedding at Cana (John 2:1–11),
- healing the royal official's son in Capernaum (4:46–54),
- healing the paralytic at the pool of Bethesda in Jerusalem (5:1–15),
- feeding the five thousand in Galilee (6:5–14),
- walking on water (6:16–24), and
- healing the man blind from birth (9:1–7).

As Ellis notes, apart from the account of the crucifixion, Jesus' raising of Lazarus is "the longest continuous narrative in the gospels. The incident occurred shortly before the Passover at which Jesus was crucified, and it is presented as prelude to that event . . . in the case of Lazarus Jesus wished to clarify the meaning of his healing power and of his claims to be the life-giver. Therefore, he delayed until Lazarus died." Once that happened, Lazarus' sisters' grief gave way to resignation. Then Jesus came. His was the calm confidence of one who knew the mission given him by the Father and who acted in the assurance of that knowledge.

> The meaning of the miracle (11:17–27) is revealed before the event itself is related (11:28–44). Martha expects her brother to rise from the grave 'at the last day', and she accepts Jesus' messianic role in that great event. But both Martha and Mary fail to see the implications *for the present* of the mission and person of Jesus. They sigh, "If you had been here" (11:21, 32). Jesus replies in effect: I *am* here. In the presence of Jesus...[death's] finality gives way to the finality of Jesus' life-giving word...[Lazarus'] resurrection is presented *as a prototype of the future resurrection in which death itself will die* (emph. added)[16].

At Jesus' command, Lazarus emerges from the tomb alive, and friends unbind his burial cloths. Lazarus's "unbinding" signifies the victory that Christ

---

15. Lazarus is both literally and spiritually delivered from the cords of death, darkness, and decay that bound him only moments before.
16. Ellis, *World of St. John*, 70–71.

has won for Lazarus and his sisters over death, grief, and hopelessness. Jesus restores Lazarus to life, returning his dear friend to family and community. Messiah's power brings shalom to a village that only minutes before was consumed by mourning.

Jesus broke up every funeral he met (by raising the would-be deceased!).

John's Gospel leaves no doubt that our Savior breaks and conquers death by the word of his power. What does this tell us about the future we have in him? Because of the cross and Jesus' own resurrection, death itself will die. What a prospect.

Hallelujah and Amen!

* * *

VERSES 45-57

45 Then many of the Jews who had come with Mary and saw what He did believed in Him;
46 But some of them went to the Pharisees and said to them the things which Jesus did.[17]
47 So the chief priests and the Pharisees gathered the Sanhedrin together. And said, "What do we do, since this man is doing many signs?
48 If we forgive him this thing, everyone will be believe him, and the Romans will come and will take away our place and our nation."[18]
49 But a certain one of them, Caiaphas, being the chief priest that year, said to them, "You know nothing;
50 Nor do you consider that it is better for you that one man die on behalf of the people than the whole nation be destroyed."[19]
51 But this he did not speak from himself, but being chief priest that year he prophesied that Jesus was about to die for the people,
52 And not for the people alone but so that the children of God scattered abroad would be gathered into one.[20]

---

17. The opposition Jesus faces in Jerusalem seems to grow inexorably.

18. The Jewish leaders' unbelief causes them to misperceive Jesus in worldly terms as a political threat.

19. Caiaphas the consummate cynic in effect proposes that Jesus be made a scapegoat for all Israel and as such be given up "for the people," with the actual purpose of preserving the Jewish religious establishment's monopoly on power.

20. John sees what Caiphas in his own "prophecy" does not: Jesus' atoning sacrifice as

The Gospel of John

53 So from that day on they resolved to kill Him.

54 As a result Jesus no longer was walking openly among the Jews but went from there to the region near the wilderness, to a town called Ephraim, and there He stayed with the disciples.

55 Now the Passover of the Jews was at hand, and many went up to Jerusalem from the country[21] for the Passover in order to purify themselves.

56 So they were looking for Jesus and standing in the temple were saying to one another, "What do you think? That He will not come to the Feast?"[22]

57 And the chief priests and Pharisees gave orders that anyone who knew where He was should report, so that they might arrest Him.

---

the once-for-all Blessed Pascha is not only for "the people" (the Jews), but for all God's children scattered abroad (not only the Jewish Diaspora, but also gentiles). Jesus is to bring "other sheep" not belonging to the Jewish fold and join them into one flock, with one shepherd (John 10:16) (Bruce, *Gospel of John*, 251).

21. The term here could signify "the region" near the desert, including the village of Ephraim, where Jesus was staying.

22. Talk of Jesus including as a result of His raising of Lazarus to life continues to dominate the crowds' conversations in the Temple.

12

John Chapter 12

VERSES 1-33

1 Then Jesus, six days before the Passover, came to Bethany,[1] where Lazarus was, the one whom Jesus raised from the dead.
2 Then they made supper for Him there, and Martha was serving, and Lazarus was one of those reclining at the table with Him.
3 Then Mary took a pound[2] of expensive ointment of pure nard and anointed Jesus' feet and wiped His feet with her hair; and the house was filled with the fragrance of the ointment.
4 And Judas Iscariot, one of His twelve disciples, the one about to betray Him, said,
5 "Why was this ointment not sold for 300 denarii and [the money] given to the poor?"
6 He said this not because the poor were a concern to him, but because he was a thief and having charge of the moneybag he stole from the contents.

---

1. In going to Bethany, Jesus now draws closer to Jerusalem. John marks carefully in the narrative how Jesus steadily approaches the hour of his trial, suffering, and ultimate victory.

2. The Greek word *litra* corresponds to about half a liter. The lavish extravagance of Mary's gesture cannot be overstated. "The outpouring of all this expensive perfume was extravagant enough, but for a woman to let down her hair and wipe a man's feet with it would have been at least as extraordinary in the eyes of that company [the group at supper] as it would be for us on a comparable occasion, and probably more so" (Bruce, *Gospel of John*, 256). This detail from the dinner is recorded only by John (Bernard, *Exegetical Commentary*, 2:418).

7 Then Jesus said, "Let her be, so that she may keep it for the day of preparation for My burial.
8 For the poor you always have with you, but you do not always have Me."

9 Then a large crowd of the Jews knew that He was there came, not only on account of Jesus, but also so that they might see Lazarus the one He raised from the dead.
10 And the Chief Priests resolved that they might kill Lazarus,
11 Since many of the Jews because of him were going away and were believing in Jesus.

12 The next day the great crowd that had come for the Feast, hearing that Jesus was coming to Jerusalem
13 Took palm branches and went out to meet Him, crying out,

> "*Hosanna;*
> *Blessed is He who comes in the Name of the* Lord,
> *Even the King of Israel.*"[3]

14 And Jesus finding a young donkey sat on it, as it is written,
15   "*Do not fear, Daughter of Zion,*
  Behold Your King comes,
  Sitting on a donkey's colt!"[4]

---

3. The people going out to meet Jesus quote Ps 118:26 as they cheer, with a clearly messianic overtone via the additional attribution of the "King of Israel." In God's providential plan, of course, Christ is not the "political" Messianic Ruler the crowd is crying out for (for deliverance from Rome), but something far better. At the same time, it is this public acclamation of Jesus as the King of Israel that later becomes the basis for charges against him before Pilate (see John 18:33) (Bernard, *Exegetical Commentary*, 2:425).

4. John abridges Zech 9:9–10:

> "Rejoice greatly, O daughter of Zion!
>   Shout aloud, O daughter of Jerusalem!
> Behold, your king comes to you,
>   triumphant and victorious is he,
> Humble and riding on a donkey,
>   on a colt, the foal of a donkey,
> I will cut off the chariot from Ephraim,
>   and the war horse from Jerusalem,
> And the battle bow shall be cut off,
>   and he shall command peace to the nations;
> His dominion shall be from sea to sea,
>   and from the River to the ends of the earth."

John Chapter 12

16 His disciples did not recognize these things at first, but when Jesus was glorified then they remembered these things that were written about Him and were done to Him.
17 Then the crowd that was with Him when He called Lazarus from the tomb and raised him from the dead continued to bear witness.
18 It was because of this the crowd met Him, that they heard of this sign that He had done.
19 So the Pharisees said to each other, "Look, you are gaining nothing; behold, the world has gone after Him."

20 And there were some Greeks among those had gone up to worship at the feast.
21 These then went to Phillip from Bethsaida of Galilee and asked him saying, "Sir, we want to see Jesus."
22 Phillip went and told Andrew, and Andrew with Phillip came and spoke to Jesus.
23 And Jesus answered them saying, "The hour has come for the Son of Man to be glorified.
24 Truly truly I say to you, unless a grain of wheat falls to the ground so that it may die, it alone remains; but if it dies, it bears much fruit.
25 The one who loves his life will lose it, and the one who hates his life in this world will keep it for eternal life.
26 If anyone serves Me, he must follow Me; and where I am, there also my servant will be; whoever serves Me, the Father will honor."

27 "Now My soul is troubled, and what shall I say? Father, save Me from this hour? But for this reason I have come unto this hour.
28 Father, glorify Thy Name." Then came a voice from heaven, "I glorified it and will glorify it again."
29 Then those standing in the crowd and hearing it were saying, "It has thundered"; others were saying, "An angel has spoken to him."
30 Jesus answered and said, "This voice was not for My sake but for yours.

The final line prefigures worldwide sovereignty from Zion's king. It is doubtful the pilgrims in Jerusalem appreciated the meaning of Jesus' action in riding on a donkey, the establishment of peace (with God and among humanity) he was inaugurating, or the sacrificial path by which God's true kingdom would be realized for Israel and the entire world. See Bruce, *Gospel of John*, 260.

31 Now is the judgment of this world, now the rule of this world will be cast out.
32 And I, when I am lifted up from the earth, will draw all people to myself."
33 And He was saying this to signify what kind of death He was about to die.

* * *

REFLECTION: "WHEN I AM LIFTED UP, I WILL DRAW ALL PEOPLE TO MYSELF"

Christ's cross invites all peoples—without distinction—to salvation though faith in him. God's gracious gift of salvation through his Son's death and resurrection leaves for each person the decision to receive or reject him. The Father's love does not, and will not, compel.
Facing the cross, we each have our own decision to make about Jesus.

Jesus makes clear in 12:32–33 that it is precisely in his crucifixion, his being 'lifted up' on the cross, that salvation is sealed for us. The church fathers can help us to plumb the simple yet deep meaning of the cross:

> "...he allowed those who were wiser to understand that he would suffer *for all and on behalf of all*" (emph. added).[5]
>
> "...he took up humanity into himself, the invisible becoming visible, the incomprehensible being made comprehensible, the impassible becoming capable of suffering and the Word being made human—thus summing up all things in himself; so that as in super-celestial, spiritual and invisible things, the Word of God is supreme, so also in things visible and corporeal he might possess the supremacy, and, taking to himself the pre-eminence, as well as constituting himself head of the Church, *he might draw all things to himself at the proper time*" (emph. added).[6]

Preeminent in all things (Col 1:18), Christ through his incarnation and sacrificial death sums up all things to himself:

> For in Him all the fullness of God was pleased to dwell,
> And through Him to reconcile to Himself all things, whether on earth or in heaven,
> Making peace by the blood of His Cross (Col 1:19–20).

Jesus came to seek and save the lost (Luke 19:10), reflecting God's desire that no one should perish (2 Peter 3:9). Intrinsic to his incarnation as the Son of

---

5. Cyril, *Commentary on John*, 2:109.
6. Daley, *God Visible*, 70. A translation of *Against Heresies* by Irenaeus of Lyons.

God is his mission to suffer and die for the life of the (entire) world. Because of his perfect, sacrificial love, Jesus' death is sufficient to save everyone:

> "And you, who once were alienated and hostile in mind by evil deeds,
> He has now reconciled in His body of flesh by His death,
> In order to present you holy and blameless and above reproach before Him" (Col 1:22).

Not only this, but at his *parousia*, creation itself will be redeemed in the new heaven and the new earth (Rom 8:19–25; Eph 1:10; Rev 21:1). Thus in the cross, we find the axis of history, and the key to God's new creation in humanity and heaven and earth itself.

Thanks be to God for His mercy. "All people" includes me, and all the people that in my hypocrisy I would not love easily.

* * *

VERSES 34-50

34 Then the crowd answered Him, "We heard from the Law that the Christ remains forever. How do you say that it is necessary for the Son of Man to be lifted up? Who is this Son of Man?"
35 Then Jesus answered them, "Yet a little while the Light is with you. Walk while you have the Light, so that the darkness does not come upon you. For the one walking in darkness does not know where he is going.
36 While you have the Light, believe in the Light, so that you may become sons of Light." [7] Jesus spoke these things, and departing He was be hidden from them.

> 7. "Who is this Son of Man?" Jesus neither answers the question nor explains himself further. Instead, he repeats his earlier stark warning (7:33, 9:4) that he will not be with them much longer, and indirectly identifies himself as God's light to whom all people should turn and believe. See Bernard, *Exegetical Commentary*, 2:444.
> The antithesis between darkness and light is "one of the most characteristic features" of John's writings in the New Testament. "In the prologue to the Gospel, the Logos is the light which, coming into the world, provides illumination for all" and is "the light which shines in the midst of the darkness and is not overcome by it" (John 1:4–9). Later in the Gospel, Jesus is the "light of the world"—by following him people "enjoy 'the light of life' instead of walking in darkness (John 3:19–21) . . . In [1 John], God is said to be light, and those who are truly his children will 'walk in the light' (1 John 1:5ff). That is to say, God is the fountain of all holiness and righteousness, goodness and truth, and his children's lives are marked by these qualities" (Bruce, *Gospel of John*, 269). God's light shines in and through Jesus, so that we can know God, and understand ourselves and our fraught

37 But even though he had done so many signs before them, they did not believe in Him,
38 So that the words of the prophet Isaiah were fulfilled, who said,

> Lord, who believed our report?
> And to whom has the arm of the Lord been revealed?[8]

39 Therefore they could believe, for again Isaiah said,
40
> He has blinded their eyes
> And hardened their hearts,
> Lest they would see with the eyes
> And know with the heart and turn,
> And I would heal them.[9]

41 Isaiah said these things because he saw His glory, and spoke concerning him.[10]
42 Nevertheless actually many also from among the rulers believed in Him, but because of the Pharisees did not confess Him lest they be put out of the synagogue,
43 For they loved the glory of men more than the glory of God.

44 Then Jesus cried out and said, "The one who believes in Me believes not in Me but the One who sent Me.
45 And the one beholding me beholds the One who sent Me.[11]
46 I, Light, have come into the world, so that all those believing in me would not remain in darkness.
47 And if anyone should hear My words and not follow, I do not judge him; for I did not come to judge the world, but to save the world.
48 The one rejecting Me and not receiving My words has One judging him; the word that I spoke, that will judge him on the last day.
49 For I did not speak from Myself, but the One who sent Me, the Father, He has given Me a commandment about what I say and what I speak.
50 And I know that His commandment is eternal life. Therefore that which I say, just as the Father has spoken to Me, so I speak."

---

condition (our need for him) more clearly.

8. Isa 53:1.
9. See Isa 6:10.
10. See Isa 6:1ff.
11. When we see Jesus for who he truly is, we see God.

13

John Chapter 13

VERSES 1-17[1]

1 Now before the Feast of Passover, Jesus knew that His hour had come that He should depart out of this world unto the Father. Having loved His own who were in the world, He loved them to the utmost.[2]
2 And it being supper, the devil already having put into the heart of Judas Iscariot, son of Simon, to betray Him,
3 Knowing that the Father had given all things into His hand and that He came from God and was going back to God,
4 He [Jesus] rose from the meal and putting aside his garments, taking a towel wrapped it around Himself.
5 Then He poured water into the washbasin and began to wash the feet of the disciples and to wipe them with the towel wrapped around Him.
6 Then He came to Simon Peter; who said to Him, "Lord, You wash my feet?"
7 Jesus answered and said to him, "That which I am doing you do not yet understand, but you will understand later."

---

1. Chapter 13 begins an extended dinner talk with his disciples, in which we find the Lord repeatedly stressing three key themes: first, I am going to the Father; second, you are staying to continue My work and third, since you can't do it alone, I am sending you the Holy Spirit (see Fee and Stuart, *How to Read the Bible*, 311).

2. "On [His disciples Jesus] had set His love in a special degree, and in the ministry of the Upper Room that love is poured out in action and word, as in the sequel [that is, the Crucifixion] it is poured out in suffering and death" (Bruce, *Gospel of John*, 278).

8 Peter said to Him, "You will never wash my feet!" Jesus answered him, "Unless I wash your feet, you have no part with Me."

9 Simon Peter said to Him, "Lord, then not my feet only but also the hands and head!"

10 Jesus said to Him, "One who has bathed does not need to wash except the feet, but is wholly clean; and you are clean, but not all [of you]."

11 For He knew the one betraying Him. Because of this He said, "Not all of you are clean."

12 Then when He had washed their feet and taken His garments, and reclined again, He said to them,

"Do you understand what I have done for you?

13 You call me Teacher and Lord, and you speak well, for I am.

14 Therefore, if I, Teacher and Lord, washed your feet, so also you should wash one another's feet.

15 For I have given you an example, so that just as I did for you, so also you should do.

16 Truly truly I say to you, a servant is not greater than his master, nor is the one sent [lit., *apostolos*] greater than the one sending him.

17 If you understand these things, blessed are you if you do them."

* * *

REFLECTION: "DO YOU UNDERSTAND WHAT I HAVE DONE FOR YOU?"

At this moment during Passover night in the Upper Room, Peter and his colleagues don't yet understand this "last lesson" Jesus gives them. The Lord enacts humble service by setting them the unthinkable (for 1st century A.D. Hebrew culture) example of foot-washing. Scholars have noted the "solemn language" in 13:3, 5 describing the scene as Jesus' humble enactment unfolds[3]:

"Knowing that the Father had given all things into His hand and that He came from God and was going back to God . . . He began to wash the disciples' feet . . ."

But how are we to understand the foot-washing? There seems to be a two-fold meaning.

The first is *theological*—remember Luke 22:24–27, where Jesus settles a quarrel among the disciples about the nature of divine lordship and authority

---

3. Bruce, *Gospel of John*, 280.

John Chapter 13

by declaring "But I am among you *as the one who serves*." In washing the disciples' feet, Jesus shows them something profound about God's person. They see "a rare unfolding of the authority and glory of the incarnate Word, and a rare declaration of the character of the Father himself ... The foot-washing symbolizes Jesus' humbling Himself to endure the death of the Cross and the cleansing efficacy of His death for the believer."[4]

The God we worship in fact kneels before us with a basin, wearing an apron, to cleanse us from all that would stand between us and him, and us from others.

The second meaning is *practical*. Jesus sets this example so that the disciples learn to perform similar service for one another and for others.[5] In so doing, the Lord "has acted out an example which [the disciples] must be prepared to imitate."[6]

This is a beautiful, disturbing lesson.

"If you understand these things, blessed are you if you do them."

What is Jesus calling me to do today, this year, for others? Am I clear about this calling, its cost, and its blessing? Am I willing to be disrupted and/or inconvenienced, or indeed to suffer, if that's what the calling entails? Am I willing to embrace God's call, even when I don't fully know where it leads? How should this impact the way I prioritize and spend my time?

Truly following Jesus means giving up control, meeting life on God's terms rather than my own. Am I ready and willing to do that?

PRAYER

Lord, give me ears to hear, and willing hands and feet to serve others in the way you desire. Help me to discern your calling(s) on my life, and give me understanding as I serve others and serve you. Give me the tools for wise discernment, including the fact that my life isn't mine to control, it's yours to lead. In your blessed name, Amen.

* * *

---

4. Bruce, *Gospel of John*, 280–281.
5. Bruce, *Gospel of John*, 283.
6. Brown, *According to John*, 569.

VERSES 18-35

18 "I do not speak concerning all of you; for I know whom I have chosen; but in order that Scripture may be fulfilled, *'The one who eats My bread lifted up his heel against me.'*[7]

19 From now I speak to you before it takes place, so that when it happens you may believe that I AM.

20 Truly, truly I say to you, the one receiving the one whom I sent receives Me, and the One receiving Me receives the One who sent Me."

21 Saying these things, Jesus was troubled in spirit and testified, and said, "Truly truly I say to you, one of you will betray Me."

22 The disciples were looking at one another, at a loss concerning of whom He spoke.

23 One of His disciples, the one Jesus loved, was reclining on Jesus' chest.

24 Then Simon Peter beckoned to Him to ask [Jesus] of whom He spoke.

25 Then the one who was reclining on the chest of Jesus said to Him, "LORD, who is it?"

26 Jesus answered, "It is he for whom I dip a piece of bread and give to him." Then dipping a piece of bread He gave it to Judas [son] of Simon Iscariot.

27 And after the piece of bread, Satan then entered in to him. Then Jesus said to him, "That which you are doing, do quickly."[8]

28 No one reclining at the table knew why He said this to him.

29 For some thought, it was because Judas had the money bag, that Jesus told him, "Buy what we need for the feast,"[9] or, that he should give something to the poor.

30 Then taking the bread, he immediately went out. And it was night.

---

7. Quoting Ps 41:9.

8. Note Judas' passive anonymity in the narrative. He is referenced with only a pronoun and says and does nothing, other than to mutely accept Jesus' offer of the piece of bread and command to act, and then to allow Satan to possess him. He is simply a mute figure of the ultimate human betrayal at this cosmic turning point. John's witness makes clear that notwithstanding Satan's agency through Judas, it is in fact Jesus who commands Judas to act, and to perform his betrayal quickly (so that God's will, as yet neither understood or even realized by the disciples, be done). Jesus' supervening word here implements God's agency and sovereignty, even when evil would seek to do its work.

9. i.e., Passover.

31 When he had gone, Jesus said, "Now the Son of Man is glorified, and God is glorified in Him.[10]

32 If God is glorified in Him, God will also glorify Him in [God] Himself, and will glorify Him at once.[11]

33 Children, yet a little while I am with you; you will seek Me, and just as I said to the Jews[12] that, 'Where I am going, you cannot come,' I also say to you now.

34 A new commandment I give to you, that you would love one another; just as I have loved you, so also you should love one another.

35 By this everyone will know that you are My disciples, if you have love for one another."

* * *

REFLECTION: A NEW COMMANDMENT

The new commandment Jesus gives in John 13:34 projects the eternal love that exists within the Trinity into the world.

Jesus in a later setting will charge his small group saying "just as the Father has loved Me, so I have loved you. Abide in my love" (John 15:9). God's love is dynamic and generative. As Christians, we abide in Christ's love *by sharing it* with one another, not only with other believers, but with those we encounter, whether friends, family or strangers, who do not know God.

This divine love also contains the answer to Christ's call to "be perfect, therefore, as your heavenly Father is perfect" (Matt 5:48). We cannot realize perfection as conceived in human terms. True perfection only exists in divine

---

10. Jesus teaches us two truths here: First, *he* is glorified in his sacrificial death on the cross for the salvation of humanity. The verb tense in the Greek is aorist (simple past), but the meaning is future. Bernard notes that "it is a Hebrew usage to employ an aorist with prophetic anticipation of the future ... [Jesus] is One to whom the inevitable future is involved with the present, and is foreseen" (Bernard, *Exegetical Commentary*, 2:524–525). Second, *God* is glorified by the Son's fulfillment of the Father's will: "I have glorified You on earth by finishing the work that You gave me to do" (John 17:4) (see Bruce, *Gospel of John*, 293).

11. Though his disciples don't yet grasp the import of his words, Jesus again testifies that God will be glorified in his imminent death and resurrection. God is glorified in Jesus the Son of Man, when the Son, betrayed by man, is willing to face and conquer death, Satan, and the power of evil by his own death (Col 2:13–15, Heb 2:14, 1 John 3:8). Jesus' faithfulness seals his eternal witness of God's sovereignty and undying love for humanity.

12. John 7:32–34.

terms, and for this reason is realized only to the extent we mirror/reflect Jesus' sacrificial, faithful love, since the Bible teaches us that God Himself is love (1 John 4:8b).

In his evocative poem "A Valediction Forbidding Mourning" presented to his wife in 1611 before a trip to the European continent, Anglican minister and poet John Donne writes:

> Such wilt thou be to mee, who must
> Like th'other foot, obliquely runne;
> Thy firmness drawes my circle just,
> And makes me end, where I begunne.[13]

Jesus took the initiative to love me first. He "draws my circle just." Thus completed by Christ's love, how can I best show that love to people in my circle, regardless of whether they are believers?

PRAYER

Lord, heaven knows, it's not that I loved you first. Thank you for your grace and mercy in first loving me. Through your love, quicken my heart and spirit to live in love toward the people in my circle and in the wider world. You came to save all creation. Help me to remember that your plan to do this includes me. May I play my tiny part in your great work and never-ending story. Amen!

* * *

VERSES 36–38

36 Simon Peter said to Him, "Lord, where are You going?" Jesus answered: "Where I am going you are not able to follow Me now, but you will follow later."
37 Peter said to Him, "Lord, why am I not able to follow You now? I will lay down my life for you."
38 Jesus answered, "You will lay down your life for Me? Truly, truly I say to you, before the rooster crows, you will deny Me three times."

---

13. Donne, *Poems of John Donne*, 51.

14

John Chapter 14

VERSES 1-7[1]

1 "Do not let your hearts be troubled; believe in God, and believe also in Me.
2 In my Father's house there are many rooms; if it were not so, would I have said to you that I am going to prepare a place for you?
3 And if I go and prepare a place for you, I will come again and I will take you to Myself, so that where I am you may be also.[2]
4 And where I am going, you know the way."
5 Thomas said to Him, "Lord, we do not know where You are going; how can we know the way?"
6 Jesus said to Him, "I AM the Way and the Truth and Life; no one comes to the Father except through Me.
7 If you have known Me, you would also know My Father. And from now on you know Him and have seen Him."

* * *

---

1. In Chapter 14, Jesus is again emphasizing for the disciples the same themes that were mentioned in n. 201 above: Jesus is going back to the Father, whom he has now fully revealed (14:1–10), the disciples are staying to continue to his work (14:11–14), and he will return to them in the person of the Spirit (14:15–31) (Fee and Stuart, *How to Read the Bible*, 312).

2. Words of power, words of love.

REFLECTION: "YOU KNOW HIM AND HAVE SEEN HIM"

Jesus' identity with the Father is such that he can give our imperfect human understanding a complete image of who God is, and what he "looks like," calling to mind Jesus' perfect love, mercy, and sense of justice.

Truly, no one has ever seen God (John 1:18), but through Jesus, we can know and experience God in his very person. The Lord was careful to shield Moses from even the sight of his back when he passed by in his glory on the mountain (Exod 33:17ff). But with Christ, we don't need to hide in the cleft of the rock. Meeting Jesus, we are face-to-face with God. We see the Father in his true nature, perfect love embodied.

* * *

VERSES 8–21

8 Philip said to Him, "Lord, show us the Father, and it is enough for us."
9 Jesus said to him, "I have been with you all this time and still you have not known me, Philip? The one who has seen Me has seen the Father. How can you say, 'show us the Father'?
10 Do you know believe that I am in the Father and the Father is in Me? The words that I say to you I do not speak from Myself, but the Father dwelling in Me does His work.
11 Believe Me that I am in the Father and the Father is in Me. But if you do not, believe on account of the works themselves.
12 Truly, truly I say to you, the one believing in Me, he will do the works that I do and he will do greater works than these, because I am going to the Father.[3]
13 And if you ask anything in My Name, I will do it, so that the Father is glorified in the Son.
14 If you ask me anything in My Name I will do it.
15 If you love Me, you will keep My commandments;
16 And I will ask the Father and He will give you another Advocate,[4] so that He may be with you forever,

---

3. The point of Jesus' self-descriptive language of identity with God to assure the disciples that in him indeed they have seen God, and to declare that in following him, they are called to do his works and even greater works because Jesus is returning to the Father.
4. 1 John 2:1.

17 The Spirit of Truth, whom the world cannot accept, because it neither recognizes nor knows Him. You know Him, because He abides with you and will be in you.
18 I will not leave you as orphans, I will come to you.
19 Yet a little while and the world will no longer see Me, but you will see Me, and because I live you also will live.
20 On that day you will know that I am in My Father, and you are in Me and I in you.
21 The one who has My commands and keeps them, he is the one who loves Me. He who loves Me will be loved by My Father, and I will love Him and will reveal Myself to him.

* * *

REFLECTION: "HE WHO HAS MY COMMANDS AND KEEPS THEM, HE IS THE ONE WHO LOVES ME"

Obedience to Christ brings intimacy with him. We honor and show our love for Jesus by remembering and obeying (doing) what he commanded, that is, to seek and love God and to love our "neighbor"—anyone we encounter who is in need. If we recognize Jesus as our crucified and risen Lord, obedience naturally follows as the way we honor and love him with our lives.

In his 1835 work *Paracelsus*, the Victorian poet Robert Browning wrote that "God is the perfect poet." Each of us is a masterwork of God, literally a *poema* (ποίημα) in the Greek, created in his image with beauty and infinite complexity (Eph 2:10). We live out the *Imago Dei* in us when we respond to God in love for him and in service to others. Through our engagement with others (particularly those in need) and fellowship with him, Christ reveals himself to us.

> When He was at table with them, taking the bread He blessed and broke and gave to them, and their eyes were opened and they recognized Him... And they explained the things that had happened on the way and how He was known to them in the breaking of the bread (Luke 24:30–31, 35).

This process of coming to know Jesus is by no means automatic, however. Jesus makes clear in this passage that only those who "have" (that is, know) and "keep" His commands truly love him, and thereby have fellowship with him and the Father (14:21, 23b). The Greek verb translated as "keep" here, τηρέω, means to "persist in obedience, observe, fulfill" (BDAG).

I have to do something consistently to truly know Jesus, not simply "know about" him. Am I keeping his commands? This is my love for the Lord. His commands are not heavy (1 John 5:1). Our Messiah is not a taskmaster. Jesus invites us,

> "Take My yoke [of discipleship] upon you and learn from Me, for I am gentle and lowly in heart, and you will find rest for your souls. For My yoke is easy, and my burden is light" (Matt 11:29–30).

PRAYER

Lord, reveal yourself in communion with us, as we walk daily with you and use what you have given us to bless and help others. Help us we pray to live faithfully and keep your commands. Grant that we could have eyes to see where we can most constructively serve your kingdom by serving those in need, and a patient, yielded heart to remember your Word revealed to us. In your name, Amen.

* * *

VERSES 22–31

22 Judas (not of Iscariot) said to Him, "Lord, how is it that You are about to reveal Yourself to us and not to the world?"
23 Jesus answered and said to him, "If anyone loves Me, he will keep My word, and My Father will love him and We will come to him and make our home with him.
24 The one who does not love Me does not keep My words; and the word that you hear is not Mine but that of the Father who sent Me."
25 "These things I have spoken to you while I am with you.
26 And the Paraclete, the Holy Spirit, He whom the Father will send in My Name, He will teach you all things and will remind you of all that I have said to you.
27 Peace I leave with you, My peace I give to you; not as the world gives do I give to you. Do not let your hearts be troubled and do not be afraid.[5]

---

5. As we picture the scene, with Jesus' language of departure growing more and more explicit, the disciples' silence implies not only rising bewilderment but no doubt fear and anxiety also: What does Jesus mean? How could He be leaving us? Why now?

John Chapter 14

28 You heard me say, 'I am going away and I will come to you.' If you loved Me you would rejoice that I am going to the Father, because the Father is greater than I.[6]

29 And now I have told you beforehand what is to be, so that when it happens you will believe.

30 I will not speak with you much longer, for the ruler of the world is coming; and upon Me he has claim,

31 But so that the world may know that I love the Father, just as the Father has commanded Me, so I do.[7]

Arise, let us go from here."[8]

---

6. Jesus is returning to glory on high with the Father, from whom he has been sent. Jesus has made plain that God's authority is greater than his. The one who is sent is not greater than the one who sent Him (John 13:16) (see Bruce, *Gospel of John*, 306). The disciples ought to rejoice, if they understood this and the blessing of peace and encouragement present to them henceforth in the person of the Holy Spirit.

7. Jesus' obedience is our model and standard.

8. Thus, Jesus enters into his trial and passion.

15

John Chapter 15

VERSES 1-10

1 "I am the true vine and My Father is the vine-dresser.
2 Every branch in Me not bearing fruit He takes away, and every one bearing fruit He prunes[1] so that it might bear abundant fruit.
3 You already are clean through the word that I have spoken to you.
4 Abide in Me, and I in you. Just as the branch cannot bear fruit from itself if it does not remain in the vine, neither can you, unless you abide in Me.
5 I am the Vine, you are the branches. The one abiding in Me and I in him, this one bears much fruit, because without Me you can do nothing.[2]
6 If anyone does not abide in Me, he is thrown away like the branch and withers; and they will gather these and throw them into the fire, and burned.
7 If you abide in Me and My words abide in you, whatever you wish, ask, and it will be unto you.[3]
8 In this My Father is glorified, that you bear much fruit and become My disciples.

---

1. That is, "cuts clean," or prunes off all barren twigs, leaves, etc., that do not contribute to the life of the branch or its production of good fruit.

2. No ministry or service can be fruitful, unless centered and rooted in Christ.

3. As Christ's words 'make their home' and dwell in us (because we mark and call them often to mind, living by them), we find ourselves in close communion with the Lord. In that, we may also see our prayers having been freely asked, freely answered. But God of course isn't a spiritual vending machine. We must ask first always, 'Thy will be done.'

9 As the Father loved me, so I have loved you; abide in My love.[4]

10 If you keep My commands, you will abide in My love, just as I have kept My Father's commands and abide in His love."[5]

* * *

REFLECTION: ABIDE WITH ME

"Abide with Me" was the closing song we sang at my mother's memorial service. The beautiful melody and strong-versed theology of this high, elegiac Scottish hymn brings tears to my eyes every time I sing it.

Written in 1847 by Anglican minister Henry Francis Lyte as he was dying of tuberculosis, the hymn's opening stanza speaks of the preciousness and undoubted frailty of our earthly life:

> Abide with me! Fast falls the eventide;
> The darkness deepens; Lord, with me abide!
> When other helpers fail and comforts flee,
> Help of the helpless, oh, abide with me.[6]

Facing the prospect of his own death on the night he was betrayed, the Lord calls the disciples, and all believers, to "abide" in His love. The Greek verb is μένω, meaning to remain, stay or continue.

My own journey with cancer teaches me that the nature of abiding is to *continue* in the love with Jesus that we who call him teacher and Lord are already in. It's not complicated, though I often make it so. I am petulant and grow impatient. I want the disease to end. I'm sick of seeing oncologists and neuro- and immuno-specialists, of having to go back on chemotherapy, of taking all the supplements. Some days it feels hard to continue fighting.

But we have only to remember where we already are—that we are his, he is ours—and act accordingly. As Dallas Willard said, "I have God, and he has the provisions. Tomorrow it will be the same... I simply ask God today for what I need."

So I just go on with God each day, no matter what. As a branch, I am joined to him and draw my life from him alone (John 15:5).

---

4. Christ is our assurance in all things.

5. Consider the relationship of the Son to the Father. Jesus' obedience ("just as I have *kept*") is expressed in the perfect tense, indicating the accomplished fact of his complete and perfect love for the Father as Jesus inexorably approaches Gethsemane and Golgotha.

6. Lyte, "Abide with Me," verse 1.

The Gospel of John

PRAYER

Blessed Lord, this day, may I remember, mark and draw strength from your connection with me and my connection to you. Abide with me. Let me even harken to you, as Paul did when he wrote "... let us fix our eyes Jesus, the author and perfecter of our faith" (Heb 12:2). The life I need and the fruit I would bear is given only by you, the true Vine.

> I need Thy presence every passing hour:
> What but Thy grace can foil the tempter's power?
> Who like Thyself my guide and stay can be?
> Through cloud and sunshine, oh, abide with me.
>
> I fear no foe, with Thee at hand to bless:
> Ills have no weight, and tears no bitterness.
> Where is death's sting? Where, grave thy victory?
> I triumph still, if Thou abide with me.[7]

* * *

VERSES 11-13

11 "I have said these things to you so that My joy may be in you and that your joy may be complete.
12 This is My commandment, that you may love one another just as I have loved you.
13 No one has greater love than this, that he lay down his life for his friends."

* * *

REFLECTION: NO GREATER LOVE

In these last moments with his disciples, Jesus doesn't speak in grand theological categories. His is the simple language of love and friendship. As confused as the disciples were at the time (and indeed as we often are!), Jesus' call goes straight to the heart: you are my friends, I love you, and I will lay down

---

7. Lyte, "Abide with Me," verses 3–4.

my life for you. The reason is only that I love you and such is needed to secure the greatest possible good for you.

The God of the universe, "the One who dwells in unapproachable light" (1 Tim 6:16; thank God that He wishes His light to be perceived by mortal eyes [Ambrose]), affirms that he is our friend who loves us above all others. So much so that he would partake of death itself in order to shatter its power and the yoke of our sin. Hallelujah!

* * *

VERSES 14–27

14 "You are my friends if you do that which I am commanding you.
15 No longer do I say you are servants, since the servant does not know what his master is doing; but you I have called friends, because all which I heard from the Father I have made known to you.
16 You did not choose Me, but I chose[8] you and appointed you that you should go and bear fruit and that your fruit might remain, so that whatever you ask the Father in My Name He may give to you.
17 These things I am commanding you, that you love one another.[9]

18 If the world hates you, know that it hated Me before you.
19 If you were of the world, the world would love you as its own; but since you are not of the world, rather I have chosen you from out of the world, because of this the world hates you.
20 Remember the word that I spoke to you: a servant is not greater than his master.[10] If they persecuted Me, they will persecute you also; if they kept My word, they will also keep yours.
21 But these things they will do unto you on account of My name, because they do not know the One who sent me.

---

8. The Greek aorist (simple past) verb here is ἐξελεξάμην (*exelezamen*), literally "I called [you] forth."

9. Reiterating the command first given in v. 12, thus framing this sub-pericope of Jesus' teaching. As we fulfill Jesus' call to go and bear "the fruit that remains," his unifying commandment is "love one another"—we should do all things in love.

10. See 13:16. The disciples can expect no better treatment from the world than that which Jesus received (NICNT).

22 If I had not come and spoken to them, they would have not had sin; but now they have no excuse concerning their sin. [11]

23 The one who hates Me also hates My Father.

24 If I had not done the works among them that no one else did, they would not have sin; but now they have seen and have hated both Me and My Father.

25 But [it was] so that the world written in their law may be fulfilled, that 'they hated me without reason.'

26 When the Helper that I will send to you from the Father comes, the Spirit of Truth who proceeds from the Father, He will testify concerning Me.[12]

27 And you also will testify, because you are with me from the beginning."

---

11. The world's sin comes to expression in its rejection of Jesus as Savior-Messiah, and consequently of God the Father (NICNT). Jesus' coming as righteousness personified reveals immediately the sin of Israel's religious leaders.

12. Even in the face of persecution, Jesus provides the blessed Spirit of Truth. God always equips His disciples with what they need to minister His word.

16

John Chapter 16

VERSES 1-7

1 "I have spoken these things to you so that you will not stumble.[1]
2 They will make you outcasts from the synagogues; indeed, the hour is coming when everyone who kills you will think that they are offering worship to God.
3 And they will do these things because they know neither the Father nor Me.
4 But I have said these things to you so that when their hour comes you may remember that I told you about them. These things I did not speak of to you from the beginning, because I was with you.[2]
5 But now I am going to the One who sent me, and no one among you asks Me, where are You going?
6 But since I have spoken these things to you, sorrow has filled your hearts.[3]

---

1. That is, to stumble into disbelief or take offense at God, when trouble comes.

2. While Jesus was with the disciples, he was their immediate protector and could deflect to himself attacks that were aimed at them. He continues to do so even when being arrested (see John 18:8-9). From now, though, things would be different. Jesus would no longer with them in the same way (physically), and they would be direct targets (Bruce, *Gospel of John*, 318).

3. Jesus completely understands the disciples' hearts. Hagar recognized God's nature when she named him after meeting him in the desert in her affliction as a God who sees: "So [Hagar] called the name of the LORD who spoke to her, 'You are a God of seeing', for she said, "Truly here I have seen Him who looks after me" (Gen 16:13). Being of the Father, the Son naturally sees as the Father sees, in love.

7 But I tell you the truth, it is to your benefit that I go away.[4] For unless I go, the Paraclete will not come to you; but if I go, I will send Him to you."

* * *

> REFLECTION: I WILL SEND HIM TO YOU
>
> Jesus' words in 16:7 are clear: He is leaving, but there is also a blessing for the disciples. In the mystery of the God's economy, Jesus' return to the Father opens the way for Him to send the Holy Spirit.
>
> Christ's promise is fulfilled in Acts 1–11, as the Spirit's anointing leads to spontaneous declaration of the Gospel in the local languages of God-fearing Jews gathered in Jerusalem to celebrate the Feast of Weeks. In a wondrous "repeal of the curse of Babel" (NICNT), these pilgrims in Jerusalem for *Shavout*, celebrating the wheat harvest, hear witness of the "mighty works of God" (τὰ μεγαλεῖα τοῦ θεοῦ; Acts 2:11) through Christ in their "home" languages, be they Persian, "Asian" (Turkish), Northern African, or Roman.
>
> Here we witness the first wave of the Gospel travelling to the ends of the earth, for the deliverance of humanity and the glory of God. The progress by his mercy continues to this day. Praise God.
>
> (Written on Pentecost, Sunday May 23, 2021)

* * *

VERSES 8–33

8 "And when He comes He will call out the world concerning sin and righteousness and judgment;[5]
9 Concerning sin, because they do not believe in Me;
10 Concerning righteousness, because I am going to the Father[6] and you will no longer behold Me;

---

4. Of course as yet none of the disciples is able to either accept or understand this truth. I doubt I'd be any different.

5. The righteousness in view is that of Jesus Himself. "The Syriac [version] . . . has (at v. 8) 'He will reprove the world in its sins and about *His* righteousness.' This brings out that the δικαιοσύνη of which the world will be 'convinced' to its shame is the δικαιοσύνη of Christ" (Bernard, *Exegetical Commentary*, 2:507). The Spirit's ministry is as counsel to the prosecution: he bears witness that the world's rejection of is now exposed as sin (v. 9).

6. "Absolute righteousness could be revealed only in the Risen Christ. With the Passion, His Revelation of the Father [and God's surpassing, eternal love for every sinner]

John Chapter 16

11 And concerning judgment, because the ruler of this world is judged.[7]

12 I have many things still to say to you, but you are not able to bear [them] yet.[8]

13 But when He comes, the Spirit of Truth, He will guide you into all truth; for He will not speak from Himself, but everything that He hears He will speak and He will declare to you the things to come.

14 He will glorify Me, because He will receive what is Mine and declare it to you.[9]

15 Whatever the Father has is Mine; because of this I said that He [the Holy Spirit] receives [it] from Me and declares [it] to you.[10]

16 A little while longer and you will no longer see Me, and again in a little while you will see Me."

17 Therefore from among His disciples they were saying to one another, "What is this that He says to us, 'A little while and you will not see Me, and again in a little while you will see Me?', and, 'because I am going to the Father'?"

18 They were saying, "What is this [that He says], 'a little while'? We do not know what He is saying."

19 Knowing that they wished to ask Him, Jesus said to them, "Concerning this do you ask one another because I said, 'A little while you will no longer behold Me, and again [after] a little while you will see Me?'

---

was completed . . . henceforth the Paraclete was to convince the world of the Perfect Righteousness which is in Christ revealed and made accessible to men" (Bernard, *Exegetical Commentary*, 2:507).

7. God's judgment of Satan's bankrupt rebellion and hatred is sealed in Jesus' victory on the cross and resurrection.

8. The coming of Jesus' word to his followers occurs in the midst of persecution by the world, requiring patience and faith.

9. Notice the blessed "economy" of the Trinity. The Holy Spirit who is both of God and the very person of God's own expression, speaks only what the Father has revealed. As he does so, the Spirit glorifies Jesus and convicts the world and the wisdom of all its ages. Here, we see the Spirit's power as the one expressing real truth, found only in the person of Jesus.

10. The Holy Spirit's manifold ministry includes: teaching the disciples all things (14:26), bearing witness to Jesus (15:26), exposing the world's error (16:8), guiding the disciples in the way of all truth (16:13), declaring to them the things to come (16:14), and glorifying Jesus (16:14). He glorifies Christ "by unfolding clearly the meaning of His person and work" (Bruce, *Gospel of John*, 321).

20 Truly, truly I say to you that you will weep and mourn, but the world will rejoice; you will grieve, but your grief will turn into joy.
21 When a woman gives birth she has pain, because her hour has come. But when the child is born, she no longer remembers the distress on account of the joy that a human being has been born into the world.
22 And you therefore now indeed have sorrow. But I will see you again, and your hearts will rejoice, and no one will take your joy from you.
23 And on that day you will not ask Me anything. Truly, truly I say to you, whatever you ask the Father in My name, He will give to you.
24 Until now you have not asked anything in My name; ask and you will receive, so that your joy may be complete.

25 I have spoken these things to you in parables; the hour is coming when I will no longer speak to you in parables, but I will tell you plainly about the Father.[11]
26 In that day you will ask in My Name; and I do not say to you that I will ask the Father for you.
27 For He the Father loves you, because you have loved Me and believed that I came from God.
28 I came from the Father, and have come into the world; again I am leaving the world and am going to the Father."
29 The disciples said to Him, "Behold, now you are speaking plainly and no longer in parables.
30 Now we know that You know all things and do not need anyone to ask You; by this we believe that You have come from God."
31 Jesus answered them, "Now you believe?
32 Behold the hour is coming and has come when you will be scattered each to his own and you will leave Me alone. But I am not alone, for the Father is with Me.
33 I have spoken these things to you so that in Me you might have hope. In the world you will have tribulation; but take heart, I have overcome the world."

---

11. In the Upper Room, Jesus had used metaphor of the vine and the vine-dresser (15:1–8) and the figure in v. 21 of the woman in childbirth. Now in his remaining time with the disciples, he speaks directly and plainly (Bruce, *Gospel of John*, 324).

John Chapter 16

*   *   *

REFLECTION: "TAKE HEART, I HAVE OVERCOME THE WORLD"

Jesus doesn't mince words when he "speaks plainly" (v. 29) with the disciples. He tells them they will all be scattered and leave him alone. They will have trouble. Faith in God is not a shield from "tribulation"—whether persecution or other trouble (disease, relational, financial). This is the reality in our beautiful, broken world. The form may vary, but we will meet hardship on the path of faith, just as the first disciples did.

But on the same path is Christ himself. The world that inflicts tribulation is his enemy as well as ours. The cross marks his victory over the world and its trials. We share in Jesus' victory.[12] By his victory on the cross, Jesus stands as our hope in all things.

Having been a faithful former practitioner, I can attest that the self-salvation strategies we default to all eventually run their course and fail us. Only Christ's conquest of "the world"—including the utter falsehood of all of our pride, obsession with glory, and a sexualized self-identity, other forms of idolatry and "therapeutic," mindless consumption—is eternal, complete and all-sufficient. The only identity we have that is true is the one given to us from the beginning by God.

In Jesus, we let go of pretense since we lack nothing, and with him our victory is complete.

PRAYER

Father, help me cultivate the attitude of mind to mark and hold close the power of your love for us in Christ. Thank you that Messiah has gone before us to undo and redeem all our categories of pretense, and to stand by us in battles that are too big for us to fight alone. Give me a humble heart able to hear and obey. Amen.

*   *   *

---

12. Bruce, *Gospel of John*, 326.

17

John Chapter 17

VERSES 1-5

1 Jesus said these things and lifting His eyes unto heaven said, "Father, the hour has come. Glorify Your Son, so that the Son might glorify You,[1]
2 Just as You gave Him authority over all flesh so that everyone You have given to Him, He might give to them eternal life.
3 And this is eternal life, that they might know You the only true God, and Jesus Christ, whom You sent.[2]

> 1. Chapter 17 records the longest prayer of Jesus in Scripture, the Prayer of Consecration. Church father Cyril of Alexandria in the fifth century speaks of Jesus in this chapter "as a high priest making intercession on our behalf." As our faithful high priest, Jesus not only offers the ultimate sacrifice to God (himself), he is also the "one who stands before the throne of God making intercession for us" (Brown, *Gospel According to John*, 747). Recall Heb 7:24-25:
>
>> "[Jesus] holds His priesthood permanently, because He continues forever. Consequently, He is able to save to the uttermost those who draw near to God through Him, since He always lives to make intercession for them."
>
> In fact, "Glorify Your Son" is the only personal intercession in the entire prayer. Jesus cares not for the glory of the world with which Satan tried to tempt him (Luke 4:5-6). He prays rather "that the Father may 'glorify' Him in His impending Passion." This isn't simply a prayer for support in trial, as a martyr might pray, but for "the divine acceptance of His sacrifice by the Father, the sealing of His mission as complete" (Bernard, *Exegetical Commentary*, 2:560).
>
> 2. The subjunctive here (that they "might know—"γινώσκωσιν"—you, the only true God") describes the goal and essence of eternal life, only possible through Christ. This life is the intimate "knowledge" described in 1 Cor 13:12 ("but when perfection comes ... then we see face to face. Now I know in part; then I shall know fully even as I have

4 I glorified You on earth by completing the works You gave to Me to do.
5 And now glorify Me, Father, with Yourself, with the glory of Your presence that I had with you before the world existed.

* * *

REFLECTION: "THE GLORY OF YOUR PRESENCE"

In John 17:5, Jesus asks for reunion with the Father in the same glory that he had with God in the Trinity, before all time or any created thing.

John implicitly evokes here his Gospel's arresting opening image—"the Word was with God and the Word was God" (1:1). John clearly affirms Christ's eternal preexistence with God and the Spirit in the pre-incarnate Godhead. Note how God's glory is *relational*—Jesus both dwells in and embodies the Father's eternal glory, and in his incarnation (climaxing with his passion) he reveals God's glory for humanity's repair and salvation. In our own far more modest way, we do something similar when we "show up" incarnationally in others' lives and do concrete things to help and encourage them:

> And the Word became flesh and dwelt among us, and we beheld His glory, glory as of the only Begotten from the Father, full of grace and truth (1:14).

* * *

VERSES 6–26

6 I have made Your Name known to the people whom You gave to me from the world. They were Yours, and You gave them to Me, and they have kept Your Word.
7 Now they know that all things which You have given to Me are from You;
8 Because the words that You gave to Me I have given to them, and they received [them] and know truly that I came from You and they believed that You sent Me.
9 I ask from them, not for the world do I ask but for the ones You have given to Me, because they are Yours,

---

been fully known" [ESV]). This means that by God's mercy, we can partake, albeit from a glorified but still human perspective, of something akin to Jesus' intimate love relationship with the Father in the Trinity unto all eternity, beginning on earth! In this way, our faith becomes illumination. We have spiritual "sightedness" enabled by God's living Word and reflected in loving acts of his church.

The Gospel of John

10 And all that are Mine are Yours and Yours Mine, and I am glorified in them.

11 And I am no longer in the world, but they are in the world, and I am coming to You. Holy Father, keep them in Your Name the ones You have given to Me, so that they may be one just as we are [One].[3]

12 When I was with them I was keeping them in Your Name that You have given to Me, and I have guarded them, and none of them was lost but the son of destruction,[4] so that Scripture might be fulfilled.[5]

13 And now I come to You and I say these things in the world, that they might have My joy fulfilled in themselves.

14 I have given to them Your word and the world hated them, because they are not of the world just as I AM not of the world.

15 I do not ask that You take them out of the world, but that You keep them from the evil one.[6]

16 They are not of the world just as I AM not of the world.

17 Consecrate them in the truth; Your word is truth.[7]

18 Just as You sent me into the world, so I sent them into the world;

---

3. When Jesus prays, ". . . keep them in Your Name that You have given to Me," the referenced "Name" most obviously is the one announced by the angel to Joseph, ". . . you are to give Him the name Jesus, for He will save His people from their sins" (Matt 1:21; note that in Luke's narrative, the angel Gabriel also proclaims Jesus' name to Mary, including also the attribution "Son of the Most High" in his announcement (Luke 1:21)). "Jesus" is the direct transliteration from the Hebrew יֵשׁוּעַ (an alternative form of "Joshua" יְהוֹשֻׁעַ, meaning "God saves" or "the Lord is salvation"). By his very name, Jesus signifies salvation and deliverance. Christ is God's rescue for his people out of their spiritual poverty, and from the power of sin, Satan, and death in the world. As Messiah, Jesus here prays that Christians' unity might be such that it mirrors the unity of the Father and the Son.

4. That is, Judas Iscariot.

5. See principally Ps 41:9 ("Even my close friend in whom I trusted, who ate my bread, has lifted his heel against me"), which Jesus applies to himself in John 13:18. Acts 1:20 also cites Pss 69:25 and 109:8 as other scriptures fulfilled by Judas (ESV).

6. Jesus desires that his disciples continue in the world, to fulfill the great commandment ("love the Lord your God") and great commission ("go and make disciples"), and asks that God, as they follow him, protect his flock from Satan and his attacks.

7. As Athanasius noted, by imitation of Jesus who is the personification of ultimate and perfect truth, we become "virtuous and [children of God]" (Schaff and Wace, *Nicene Fathers*, 4:404). Christ asks God to separate believers from the world by that truth.

John Chapter 17

19 And for them I consecrate Myself,[8] so that they also may be consecrated in the truth.[9]

20 I do not ask for these only, but also for those believing in Me through their word,[10]

21 so that all may be one, just as You, Father, are in me and I in You, so that these also may be in us, so that the world might believe that You sent Me.[11]

22 And I have given them the glory which You have given to Me, so that they may be one just as we are one;

23 I in them and You in Me, so that they may be made perfect in one, so that the world may know that You sent Me and that You loved them just as You loved Me.[12]

24 Father, those whom You have given to Me, I desire that where I am they may be with Me, so that they might behold My glory, which You gave to me because You loved Me before the foundation of the world.[13]

25 Righteous Father, indeed the world did not know You, but I have known You, and these have known that You sent Me.

---

8. The verse recalls Jesus' earlier testimony in 10:18 (". . . I have authority to lay it down") regarding his authority to fill a priestly role in which he is both the dedicating priest and the sacrifice itself. "In His death [Jesus] was both priest and victim" (Bernard, *Exegetical Commentary*, 2:575).

9. Jesus is dedicating himself to the Cross. Looking towards Gethsemane and Golgotha, Jesus offers himself as a sacrifice to God, that his people might be cleansed, liberated, and set apart for the purpose of being the agents of his kingdom in history. "It was not what Jesus' executioners did to Him, but what He did Himself in His self-offering, that makes His death a prevailing sacrifice 'for the life of the world (John 6:51: "And the bread that I give for the life of the world is My flesh")" (Bruce, *Gospel of John*, 334).

10. The "other sheep" in Jesus' kingdom (10:16; that is, gentiles) will be brought in the words of evangelist believers.

11. Jesus prays for the unity of all future believers as a testimony that he was sent into the world by God, to save and redeem it.

12. Christ's focus in 17:23–24 on the importance of unity among believers could not be clearer. Nothing less is at stake than the church's witness of Jesus to the world, that the world might believe.

13. Christ attests to the eternal bond of the Trinity. Jesus' glory is the love God has had for him, and by extension through him for all Christians (those given by God to Jesus), from all eternity. In the community of heaven, all those trusting in Jesus will 'behold with sustained attention' (*theorosin* is the Greek term for "behold" in 17:24) God's eternal love for the Son. As they do so, they will experience for themselves the peace, joy, and beauty of the Lord's person.

The Gospel of John

26 And I have made known Your Name to them and I will make it known, so that the love with which You loved Me may be in them and I in them."[14]

---

14. To "know God's name" or inherent nature is to know his love, which only Jesus —"as the eternal object of His Father's love"—knows. Only he understands and can "translate" for our benighted world the justice, mercy, and holiness that God has and desires to give to us through the gift of the Son (Tasker, *John*, 191).

18

John Chapter 18

VERSES 1-38

1 After saying these things Jesus went out with His disciples across the Kidron Valley where there was a garden, which He and His disciples entered.[1]
2 Now Judas His betrayer also knew the place, because Jesus often gathered with His disciples there.
3 Then Judas, bringing a detachment of soldiers, and officers from the chief priests and Pharisees, went there with lamps and torches and weapons.
4 Then Jesus, having known all things that were to come upon Him[2] went out and said to them, "Whom are you looking for?"
5 They answered Him, "Jesus the Nazarene." He said to them, "I AM" [He]. And Judas who betrayed Him was standing there with them.
6 When He said to them, "I AM" [He], they drew back and fell to the ground.[3]

---

    1. With Jesus and the disciples' entry into Gethsemane, John's crucifixion narrative begins.

    2. The perfect participle here ("having known") reflects the completeness of Jesus awareness of what lies ahead. "John is at every point careful to insist that Jesus foreknew the issues of His ministry" (Bernard, *Exegetical Commentary*, 2:585).

    How lonely it must have been for Jesus. But in the "I AM" of his self-identification to the mob, we see the power of his love. The Son would go even to the cross, knowing "everything that was coming upon Him."

    3. We see the Word of Jesus' power before those who would arrest him. Their shock and awe suggests that Jesus' captors understood fully that he was using the very name

7 Then again He asked them, "Whom are you seeking?" And they said, "Jesus the Nazarene."
8 Jesus answered, "I said to you that I AM [He]. Therefore if you are seeking Me, let these [men] go."
9 Thus was fulfilled the word that He had spoken that, "I have lost none of those whom You have given to Me."[4]
10 Then Simon Peter having a sword drew it and struck the servant of the High Priest, and cut off his right ear; the name of the servant was Malchus.
11 Then Jesus said to Peter, "Put the sword in the sheath; shall I not drink the cup that the Father has given to me?"[5]

12 Then the soldiers and the captain and the deputies of the Jewish religious leaders[6] arrested Jesus and bound Him
13 and led Him first to Annas; for he was the father-in-law of Caiaphas, who was the high priest that year;
14 And Caiaphas was the one who had advised the Jews that it would be expedient for one man to die for the people.[7]

15 And Simon Peter and another disciple were following Jesus. That disciple was known to the high priest and went with Jesus into the courtyard of the high priest,
16 But Peter stood before the door outside. Then the other disciple known to the high priest came out and spoke to the doorkeeper[8] and brought Peter in.

---

of God to identify himself: not only Jesus of Nazareth, but the One Who Is Who He Is, forever.

4. The Evangelist likely has in mind here John 17:12.

5. Jesus recognizes that "... evil can only be overcome if Jesus Himself drinks the cup of the wrath of God, and He is under a divine necessity to drink that cup alone and to drink it to the full" (Tasker, *John*, 195).

6. *Lit.*, "officers of the Jews."

7. John reports Caiphas's statement as a prophesy in 11:49–52 ("... being high priest that year he prophesied that Jesus would die for the nation, and not for the nation only, but also to gather into one the children of God who are scattered abroad"). Caiaphas's short-sighted political calculus ironically and unknowingly anticipates the cosmic watershed of the crucifixion and Jesus' atonement for humanity thereby.

8. The gender of the noun here (τῇ θυρωρῷ) is feminine, looking ahead to the "servant girl" (ἡ παιδίσκη) in v. 17.

John Chapter 18

17 Then the servant girl doorkeeper said to Peter, "Are you not one of the disciples of this man?" He said, "I am not."[9]

18 And the servants and officers were standing there having made a fire, because it was cold, and they were warming themselves.

19 Then the chief priest questioned Jesus about His disciples and about His teaching.

20 Jesus answered him, "I have spoken plainly to the world, I taught always in the synagogue and in the Temple, where all the Jews come together, and I have spoken nothing in secret.

21 Why do you ask Me? Ask those who heard what I said to them. Behold, these know what I said to them."

22 As He was saying these things, one of the officers standing nearby struck Jesus in the face saying, "Is this how you answer the high priest?"

23 Jesus answered him, "If I have spoken wrongly, bear witness concerning the wrong; and if I have spoken in the right, why do you strike Me?"

24 Then Annas sent Him bound to the high priest.

25 And Simon Peter was standing warming himself [by the fire]. Then they said to him, "Are you not one of his disciples?" He denied it and said, "I am not."

26 One of the servants of the high priest, being a relative of the one whose ear Peter cut off, said, "Did I not see you in the garden with him?"

27 Then Peter again denied it, and immediately a rooster crowed.

28 So they led Jesus from Caiaphas to the Praetorium.[10] It was early in the morning; and they did not enter the Praetorium, so that they would not be defiled but could eat the *Pascha*.[11]

---

9. Notice the ironic contrast John draws between Jesus' word of power upon meeting his captors in 18:5 ("I am He") and Peter's fearful self-negation ("I am not") as he denies Christ here.

10. This handover marks Jesus' transfer from Jewish to Roman authority. The Praetorium was the Roman prefect or governor's residence in Jerusalem. Pilate resided in Caesarea Phillipi on the Mediterranean coast, but when in Jerusalem he used the palace compound built by Herod as his headquarters (Wikipedia, "Pilate's Court"). Long identified with the Antonia Fortress located on the northwest corner of the Temple Mount, the Praetorium may have actually been at the palace built by Herod located at the Jaffa Gate at the western entrance to the Old City (ESV, 2062).

11. That is, the Passover lamb.

29 Then Pilate went out to them and said, "What charge do you bring against this man?"
30 They answered and said to him, "If this man were not doing evil things, we would not have delivered him over to you."
31 Pilate then said to them, "You take him and judge him according to your law." The Jews said to him, "It is not lawful for us to kill anyone."
32 Thus the word of Jesus might be fulfilled that He spoke foretelling by what kind of death He was about to die.[12]

33 Then Pilate again entered the Praetorium and called to Jesus and said to Him, "You are the king of the Jews?"
34 Jesus answered, "Are you saying this from yourself or did others speak to you concerning me?"
35 Pilate answered, "Am I a Jew? Your people and the High Priest handed you over to me. What have you done?"
36 Jesus answered, "My Kingdom is not of this world; if My Kingdom was of this world, my servants would have fought so that I would not have been delivered over to the Jews; but now My Kingdom is not from here."
37 Then Pilate said to Him, "Then you are a king?" Jesus answered, "You say that I am a king. Unto this I have been born and for this I have come into the world, so that I could witness to the truth. Everyone who is of the truth listens to My voice."
38 Pilate said to Him, "What is truth?"

* * *

REFLECTION: "WHAT IS TRUTH?"

Sitting amidst the cultural and moral chaos that now permeates our secularized modern society, it is tempting to hear Pilate's question to Jesus in the key of deconstructionist post-modernism ("Truth? The only genuine truth is that which I choose to define for myself," etc.).

---

12. A tool of Roman imperial subjugation, crucifixion was anathema to the Jews. The Torah taught that a hanged man was "cursed by God" (Deut 21:22–23). The "word of Jesus" here is his earlier prophesy in 12:32–33 of his impending death by crucifixion: "'And I, if I am lifted up from the earth, will draw all people to myself.' And He said this signifying by what kind of death He was about to die." The ultimate sign of God's faithful love and mercy for humanity is the forsaken death of his only begotten Son sealing salvation and restoration for the life of the world.

But to understand Pilate's question this way would be *eisegesis*—that is, reading into or imputing to the text one's own meaning, a meaning that was never present to begin with, that the original writer or speaker never intended or indeed could have even conceived of.

Our task as faithful readers and interpreters of God's Word is rather to do *exegesis*; to read and "critically... interpret the text in order to discover its *original meaning*" (emph. added)[13].

Exegetically speaking then, we could understand what Pilate says in one of two ways:

Most simply, Pilate could be seen as sardonically challenging Jesus' claims that 1) He—not Caesar, not the High Priest—is the true "witness to the truth" and 2) that all who "listen to" (obey) Jesus' voice are "of the truth" (18:37). In this light, Pilate's question is simply the voice of Imperial Rome, mocking the wild claims of a prisoner upon whom he is about to render the death sentence.

At the same time, Pilate's question could be read to carry a wistful, or even unconsciously tragic tone. Seen thus, cynic and imperial collaborator though he may be, Pilate rues his position within his apparent position of "power" but simultaneous actual lack thereof. He realizes he stands not only beneath Rome but now, apparently, also somehow subordinate to this strange rabbi, who in one breath quietly and comprehensively unmasks all of Pilate's authority and supposed claims upon his life as utterly empty and powerless without God ("You would have not authority over me at all unless it had been given you from above" [19:11]). Preoccupied as he is by self-interest and expediency, Pilate in his haste to rid himself of a troublesome case cannot grasp the "truth" of Jesus' power, and its self-giving, life-giving nature and source in the one true God-now-incarnated (1:14; 14:6).

However we interpret Pilate's question, what is clear is that Jesus speaks in categories that Pilate either cannot—or chooses not to—understand. After repeated encounters with the crowd and Jesus privately, Pilate pronounces Jesus innocent to the Jewish leaders ("I find no guilt in him" (18:38)), yet like the rich young man recounted in the Synoptic Gospels (Matt 19:16–30, Mark 10:17–31, Luke 18:18–30) remains sadly unchanged by his encounter with the Messiah.

Reading this trial transcript, how do I see Jesus? Am I able to hear and apply the truth of his word in my life? What is my response as I pray and reflect?

Pilate imagined he was leading out a sacrifice to appease a restive mob, when in fact Jesus in faithful obedience to God was allowing himself to be

---

13. See Encyclopedia Britannica, "Exegesis."

offered as the eternal Πάσχα (*Pasca*; derived from פֶּסַח [*Pesach*] in Hebrew and פַּסְחָא [*Paskha* in Aramaic], meaning Passover), in order to destroy Satan (Heb 2:14), atone for our sins (1 Peter 2:24; 1 John 1:7), and conquer death (1 Cor 15:22–26).

> Clean out the old yeast, so that you may be a new batch, for you really are unleavened. For Christ, our Passover Lamb, has been sacrificed (1 Cor 7:5).

PRAYER

Lord, help me to recognize that Jesus is the ultimate truth (John 14:6), revealed as Messiah when God offered up his own beloved Son as the eternal πάσχα (*pasca*), the "Passover Lamb," given once for my and all sins, for all time (John 1:29; 1 Peter 3:18). I pray the truth of Jesus would ever abide in my heart, soul, and mind. Amen.

* * *

VERSES 38–40

38 And saying this he again went out to the Jews and said to them, "I find no guilt in him.
39 There is a custom among you that one be released to you on Passover. Do you wish then that I release to you the King of the Jews?"
40 Again they cried out saying, "Not this one but Barabbas." Now Barabbas was a thief.

19

John Chapter 19

VERSES 1-5

1 Then Pilate took Jesus and scourged Him.
2 And the soldiers, after twisting together a crown of thorns, put it on His head and clothed Him with a purple robe,
3 And bowed before Him saying, "Hail King of the Jews!" and beat Him.
4 And again Pilate went out and said to them, "Behold, I am bringing him out to you, so that you may know that I find no basis for a charge against him."
5 The Jesus came out, wearing the crown of thorns and the purple robe.[1] And he[2] said to them, "Behold the man!"[3]

---

1. Rome, the blasphemous and demonic imperial power, clothes Jesus in caricatured vestments of royalty in an attempt to mock and belittle his true status as King of Kings and Lord of Lords. Rare and costly to produce as a dye, purple was a royal color in biblical times (Laden, "Royal Purple of David and Solomon").

2. That is, Pilate.

3. In another example of Johannine irony, Pilate's words recall the term Jesus consistently uses when referring to himself: the "Son of Man." In Caiaphas's words that "one man" is destined to "die for the people" (11:50)—and in fact as it turns out, for all people. In Hebrew or Aramaic (בר נשא, *bar nasha*), "son of man" translated would mean simply a man, or the man (NICNT). The term "Son of Man" appears twelve times in John's gospel: 1:51; 3:13, 14; 5:27; 6:27, 53, 62; 8:28; 9:35; 12:23; 13:31; in 12:34, Jesus' language is quoted back to him when the Jerusalem crowd asks him, "Who is this Son of Man?"

When Pilate cries out to the crowd, "Behold the man!" two points are noteworthy about Jesus' title as "Son of Man":

First is the fact that Jesus is a real man, and God incarnate. This is the culmination of

THE GOSPEL OF JOHN

* * *

REFLECTION: "BEHOLD THE MAN!"

How did Jesus feel facing the crowd, hearing Pilate's declamation? John's account is poignantly silent.

We can only imagine Jesus' isolation and pain as He stood before the mob, utterly alone in the knowledge of God's and humanity's complete rejection. The crowd was about to demand his crucifixion; the "cup" of His Father's wrath was before Him to drink to the dregs.

And Jesus obeyed God, for your sake and mine.

The crowd shouted its judgment and the Father turned His face away. Jesus went on alone into darkness at Golgotha. I can't conceive of a longer or more lonely road than the one Jesus had to walk, bearing the Cross, having been scourged, mocked and beaten. Because of His silent, faithful obedience to satisfy God's holy wrath and bear the weight of the world's sin, now we can walk in the light, forever forgiven and free.

By draining the cup of condemnation, Jesus saved us for Himself, from ourselves.

> "God shows His love for us in this, that while we were still sinners, Christ died for us" (Rom 5:8).

Thanks be to God, Amen.

* * *

---

the "Word becoming flesh." Indeed, Jesus became "like his brothers and sisters in every respect" (Heb 2:17), which means that unlike anything found in other world religions and contrary to heresies ranging from second century Gnosticism and Docetism to modern-day Jehovah's Witnesses, the God of the Christian faith knows our suffering (physical, relational, emotional, spiritual) in a direct and personal way.

Second, is that as Jesus stands as defendant in Pilate's court, he represents all humanity. He is the very agent of our redemption, "God for us." As Calvin writes, "it is part of our redemption" that Jesus was "arraigned before the judgment seat as a criminal, accused and condemned by the mouth of a judge to die." The charges we face at the judgment seat of God (blasphemy, in our pretension to be like God and treason, in our rebellion against Him) are in fact the charges Jesus faced at the judgment seat of Caiaphas and Pilate (NICNT, quoting *Institutes of the Christian Religion* by John Calvin, II.vi.5; Milne, *Message of John*, 273–76).

John Chapter 19

VERSES 6-42

6 When the chief priests and temple police saw Him they cried out saying, "Crucify, crucify!" Pilate said to them, "You take him and crucify him; for I find no fault in him."[4]

7 The Jews answered him, "We have a law and according to that law he ought to die, because he made himself the Son of God."[5]

8 So when Pilate heard this word, he was even more afraid.

9 And he entered the Praetorium and said to Jesus, "Where do you come from?"[6] But Jesus did not give him an answer.

10 So Pilate said to Him, "You do not speak to me? Do you not know that I have authority to release you and authority to crucify you?"

11 Jesus answered, "You would have no authority over Me whatsoever if it had not been given to you from above. Because of this the one who delivered Me over to you has greater sin.[7]

12 From this time on Pilate was seeking to release Him, but the Jews cried out saying, "If you release this man, you are not a friend of Caesar. Everyone who makes himself a king opposes Caesar."

13 Hearing these words, Pilate then brought Jesus out and sat down on the judgment seat at a place called the Stone Pavement [*lithostratos*], and in Aramaic *Gabbatha*.[8]

---

4. While the Jewish religious establishment leaders cite "the Law" (the Torah, set forth in the first five books of the Old Testament) as their prooftext for the death sentence in the next verse, Pilate finds Jesus entirely innocent. In his fear (19:8), Pilate also simply wants to be rid of the matter, and cares nothing for what happens to Jesus. Thus his words here reenact 18:31 ("Take him and judge him according to your law"), but now with added specificity: in effect, "*you* crucify him, not I" (NICNT).

5. "Whoever blasphemes the name of the LORD shall surely be put to death . . ." (Lev 24:16). Jesus' statements to the effect that he was the Son of God (see John 5:18, 8:56–58 and 10:33) were blasphemy in the eyes of the Pharisees.

6. The question could be rephrased "*Who* are you?" Pilate's streetwise cunning and fear of the supposed source of his power (Rome) renders him unable to grasp Jesus' true identity or how to deal with him. Jesus' generally silent manner, and strangely powerful words when he does answer, make Pilate uneasy, and he doesn't know what to do with him.

7. Jesus' statement about the true origin of Pilate's authority (given to him by God) puts the lie to Pilate's alleged basis for his authority (supposedly Caesar). Nevertheless, Jesus further asserts, Caiphas who hands him over to Pilate bears the greater sin: by this act, Caiphas is abusing his sacral authority as high priest and head of the Jewish religious establishment (Bruce, *Gospel of John*, 362).

8. Normally, Pilate would have conducted the whole trial of an accused like Jesus from the *bema*, or raised platform, in the Praetorium from which judgments were rendered.

14 Now it was the Day of Preparation for the Passover, at about the sixth hour.⁹ And he said to the Jews, "Behold your king!"¹⁰

15 Then they shouted out, "Away, away, crucify him!" Pilate said to them, "Shall I crucify your king?" The high priests answered, "We have no king but Caesar."¹¹

16 Then he handed Him over to them to be crucified.

So they took Jesus,

17 and bearing by Himself the cross He went out to the place called the Place of the Skull, which in Aramaic is called *Golgotha*,¹²

18 where they crucified Him, and with Him were two others, one on each side, and Jesus in the middle.

19 And Pilate also wrote an inscription¹³ and put it on the Cross, and [on] it was written

---

In this case the Jewish religious authorities' "unwillingness to contract defilement" by entering the building necessitated Pilate's moving back and forth between them, as they stood by the outer colonnade, and Jesus, whom he questioned inside the building itself (Bruce, *Gospel of John*, 363).

9. That is, noon (ESV study note).

10. Note the contrast with v. 5 ("behold the man"). Pilate's mordant sarcasm is directed at the Jews rather than Jesus (Bernard, *Exegetical Commentary*, 2:624). The truth of Pilate's statement however is deeper than he knows. John sees the deeper meaning: "Jesus, he implies, is the true king of the true Israel, of all the people of God who belong to the cause of truth and obey the voice of Him who is truth incarnate (cf. 18:37). And in the fact that these words were spoken towards midday on Passover Eve [John] implies something else: Jesus is the true paschal lamb, about to suffer death at the appropriate hour of the appropriate day for the life of His people" (Bruce, *Gospel of John*, 365).

11. The chief priests not only deny Jesus as king but in the process also reject the first tenet of Jewish theocracy, that the Lord God is their king (1 Sam 12:12) (Bernard, *Exegetical Commentary*, 2:624).

12. As attested in synoptic Gospels, Simon of Cyrene (a region in North Africa with a large Jewish population) is compelled to bear the cross for Jesus when its weight overmatches what little physical strength Jesus has left after being beaten and scourged (Matt 27:32; Mark 15:21; Luke 23:26). Here however, as he exits the Praetorium to begin his the loneliest of all walks, Christ carries his cross alone. Roman law and practice at the time required that a criminal condemned to be crucified carry his own cross (Bernard, *Exegetical Commentary*, 2:626, citing Plutarch).

Jesus "goes forth"—exiting Jerusalem proper—since executions were not allowed within the city's walls. Recall Heb 13:12: "So Jesus also suffered *outside the gate* in order to sanctify the people through His own blood" (emph. added) (Bernard, *Exegetical Commentary*, 2:626).

13. This is the "title" or *titulus* (transliterated τίτλον in the Greek), "the technical Latin name for the board bearing the name of the condemned or his crime or both, [and] is

John Chapter 19

"Jesus of Nazareth
King of the Jews."

20 Many of the Jews read this sign, because the place where Jesus was crucified was near the city; and it was written in Aramaic, Latin, and Greek.
21 Then the chief priests of the Jews were saying to Pilate, "Do not write 'the King of the Jews' but that 'He said, I am the King of the Jews.'"
22 Pilate answered, "What I have written, I have written."[14]

23 Then the soldiers, when they crucified Jesus, took His garments and divided them into four parts, one part for each soldier, and the tunic. And the tunic was seamless, woven from top to bottom.
24 Then they said to one another, "Let us not tear it, but cast lots for whose it will be"; so that Scripture might be fulfilled, which says:

***"They divided My garments among them
And for My clothing they cast lots."***[15]

The soldiers thus did these things.[16]

---

only so called by John (in Mark, it is called 'the inscription of the charge' ἡ ἐπιγραφὴ τῆς αἰτίας)" (Bernard, *Exegetical Commentary*, 2:627).

14. The Greek perfect verb tense here, "What I have written, I have written," "marks the permanence and abiding character" of Pilate's act. "Pilate was a true Roman in his respect for an official document. He was himself responsible for the phrasing of the *titulus*, and, once written and affixed to the cross, it was the expression of a legal decision. From the legal point of view he was right in refusing to alter its terms" (Bernard, *Exegetical Commentary*, 2:629). Pilate's refusal unknowingly and ironically affirms Isa 9:7, Zech 9:9 and many other prophetic references to Jesus as Israel's one true Messiah King.

15. Psalm 22:18. Jesus' own words of anguish as recorded in Matthew's (27:46) and Mark's (15:34) accounts quoting Ps 22:1 ("My God, My God, why have You forsaken me?") make clear that the Lord himself understood Psalm 22 (and indeed all of the Hebrew scriptures) as prophetically forecasting his true Messiahship as both "Son of Man" and "Son of God."

16. By custom the clothes of the executed criminal were the executioners' to claim (Carson, *According to John*, 611).
Note also:
"John finds in the words [of Psalm 28] an inspired forecast of that which was witnessed at the Crucifixion, namely the division of some garments, and the drawing of lots for one in particular . . . *John sees in all the incidents of the Passion the fulfillment of the Divine purposes disclosed in the Old Testament*, and so he says that these things happened [so that Scripture might be fulfilled]" (emph. added) (Bernard, *Exegetical Commentary*, 2:630; Bernard uses the original Greek in the bracketed language).

The Gospel of John

25 Standing by the Cross of Jesus were His mother, His mother's sister, Mary of Clopas,[17] and Mary Magdalene.[18]

26 Then Jesus beholding His mother and the disciple whom He loved standing nearby, said to His mother, "Woman, behold, your son!"

27 Then He said to the disciple, "Behold, your mother!" And from that hour the disciple took her into his own home.[19]

28 After this, Jesus, knowing that all things had now been accomplished, so that scripture might be fulfilled, said, "I thirst."[20]

29 A jar full of sour wine was standing there.[21] So putting a sponge full of sour wine on a hyssop branch, they held it to His mouth.

30 When He had taken the sour wine Jesus said, "It is finished," and bowing His head He gave up His spirit.

---

17. Likely meaning "Mary, the wife of Clopas."

18. Set against the soldiers' brutally efficient work, the women closest to Jesus "wait in faithful devotion to the One whose death they can still understand only as tragedy" (Carson, *According to John*, 615).

19. In the final moments of his earthly life, after forgiving those who had brought him to the cross (Luke 23:34) and then also ministering a word of promise to the thief beside him pleading for mercy (Luke 23:43), we see Jesus providing for the care of his mother by his beloved friend.

20. John's portrayal of the scene "forbid[s] any theory of Christ's person that does not recognize His manhood. Jesus was *thirsty* on the Cross" (Bernard, *Exegetical Commentary*, 2:636). One example of such a theory was the Gnostic heresy of docetism, which claimed that Christ's body was not human but either a phantasm or of real but celestial substance, and that therefore his sufferings were only apparent.

Note also how Ps 69:21—"... for my thirst they gave me sour wine to drink"—registers prophetically here and in the next verse (19:29).

Regarding "It is finished": Bernard makes the sound point that "τετέλεσται is not a cry of relief that it is all over; it is a shout of victory. The mission of redemption has now been perfected" (Bernard, *Exegetical Commentary*, 2:638).

21. At the wedding at Cana (2:1–11), there were six water jars. In his first miracle or "sign," Jesus turns the water in these jars to fine wine for guests to drink (2:6). The seventh wine jar recorded in John's Gospel is the one appearing here in 19:29, in very different circumstances, and at the beginning of an even greater miracle. The contrast between Cana and Golgotha could not be more striking: wedding/execution; joy and anticipation/pain, grief, and bitter hopelessness; fine wine for nuptial celebrants/sour wine for the cursed accused. Seven was symbolic for fullness and completeness in Israelite and Near Eastern culture and literature (BibleProject, "Significance of Seven"). Fittingly then, the sour wine from this seventh jar marks the perfect completion of Christ's work of redemption. After drinking it, Jesus' final words recorded by John are "It is finished" (19:30), as God's judgment of all humanity now bears down upon the Lamb of God alone.

John Chapter 19

31 Then the Jews, because it was the Day of Preparation, so that the bodies might not remain on the crosses on the Sabbath, for that day was a high Sabbath, petitioned Pilate that the legs [of the crucified] might be broken and that they might be taken away.[22]

32 Then the soldiers came and broke the legs of the first and the other crucified with Him.

33 But coming to Jesus, when they saw that He was already dead, they did not break His legs,

34 But one of the soldiers with his spear pierced His side, and at once blood and water came out.[23]

35 And he who saw this has testified, and his testimony is true, and he knows that he speaks the truth, so that you also might believe.[24]

36 For these things took place in order that the Scripture might be fulfilled,

---

22. See Deut 21:22–23: "And if a man has committed a crime punishable by death and he is put to death, and you hang him on a tree, his body shall not remain all night, but you shall bury him the same day, *for a hanged man is cursed by God. You shall not defile the land that the* LORD *your God is giving you for an inheritance*" (emph added). As further context,

> "... the usual Roman practice was to leave a corpse on its cross ... But there was no Roman law forbidding burial ... Hence, although Pilate, in ordinary circumstances, might have refused the request of the [Sanhedrin leaders], there was nothing to prevent him from granting it if he wished. And, in this case, there was the further consideration that Jerusalem, at the moment, was crowded with pilgrims who had come for the Passover, and that it was desirable to avoid a conflict between the Jews and the Roman authorities" (Bernard, *Exegetical Commentary*, 2:642).

23. John's account is faithfully anti-Docetic: "Jesus died as a fully human being with a genuine human body" (ESV note on 19:34). On Docetism, see footnote 9 on page 3 and 20 on page 130.

The other place in the New Testament where blood and water are mentioned together comes in John's first epistle, where he affirms their role in God's own testimony, through the Holy Spirit, regarding his Son:

> "This is He who came by water and blood—Jesus Christ; not by water only but by the water and the blood. [That is, the water of His baptism and the blood of His cross.] And the Spirit is the one who testifies, because the Spirit is the truth. For there are three that testify: the Spirit and the water and the blood; and these three agree. If we receive the testimony of men, the testimony of God is greater, for this is the testimony of God that He has borne concerning His Son. Whoever believes in the Son of God has the testimony in Himself." (1 John 5:6–9).

24. God always gives a witness to the truth. John is "the witness *par excellence*, whose 'testimony is true' and on whose authority the whole Gospel was written. In short, the author of the Gospel is pausing at a crucial point in the story to verify the details of Jesus' death, assuring us that he writes what he himself has seen" (Michaels, NICNT).

The Gospel of John

"His bones shall not be broken."[25]

37 And again another Scripture says,

"They looked on the one whom they had pierced."[26]

38 After these things Joseph of Arimathea,[27] being a disciple of Jesus secretly for fear of the Jews, petitioned Pilate that he might take the body of Jesus; and Pilate gave permission. So he came and took away his body.
39 And Nicodemus, the one who came to Him at first by night, came bringing a mixture of myrrh and aloes weighing 75 pounds.[28]
40 Then they took the body of Jesus and bound it in linen cloths with the spices, according to the burial custom of the Jews.
41 And at the place where He was crucified there was a garden, and in the garden a new tomb in which no one had yet been laid.
42 There, on account of it being the Day of Preparation of the Jews, and because the tomb was near, they laid Jesus.

* * *

25. According to the Torah, the bones of the Passover lamb were not to be broken (see Exod 12:46, Num 9:12). "This, to John, was a prophetic ordinance, and pointed forward to the manner of the death of Him who was the true Paschal Lamb. In this identification of Jesus with the Paschal Lamb, Paul is in agreement with John: 'Christ our Passover is sacrificed for us' (1 Cor 5:7)" (Bernard, *Exegetical Commentary*, 2:651).

26. "And I will pour out on the house of David and the inhabitants of Jerusalem a spirit of grace and pleas for mercy, so that, when they look on me, *on him whom they have pierced*, they shall mourn for him, as one mourns for an only child, and weep bitterly over him, as one weeps over a firstborn" (Zech 12:10) (emph. added).

"Behold, He is coming with the clouds, and every eye will see Him, *even those who pierced Him*, and all tribes of the earth will wail on account of Him. Even so, Amen." (Rev 1:7) (emph. added). Jesus is pouring out a spirit of grace and pleas for mercy for the house of David and those living in Jerusalem, would that they there able to receive it.

27. Although its precise location is not known, Arimathea is generally understood to have been a city of the Jews in the hill country west of Bethel (Bible Atlas, "Arimathea").

28. Like a fourth Magi, Nicodemus comes bearing a most costly gift. The sheer quantity of the spices he brings suggests a burial anointing for a king. This wholly befits Jesus' title on the cross as "King of the Jews" (Michaels, NICNT), and his identity as Israel's true, humble king whose coming riding on a donkey has been long foretold (Zech 9:9; Matt 21:5).

JOHN CHAPTER 19

REFLECTION: TWO GARDENS

Eden's garden frames a community where God and humanity dwell together as friends. Imagine! To walk with God in the cool of the evening. But with the fall, Eden becomes the site of humanity's spiritual death.

And now comes another garden, long after the fall, yet appearing "in the fullness of time" (Gal 4:4). Near Golgotha, the place of torture and death, and itself a place of burial. Near the site of history's darkest and brightest event, a refuge, a place of greenery, peace, and stillness for the unfolding of history's greatest miracle.

At Eden, what was life turned into death. In this second garden, the reversal appears: God's life breaks forth out of death, conquering it, and love breaks forth in the conquest of fear, pain, and faithlessness. Jesus by his death and resurrection restores the community that was once Eden's, reclaiming the promise of the first garden.

God's victory begins on the Cross and continues in the cool morning of the second garden with the greatest of new beginnings, Jesus' redeeming new creation.

As John records in chapter 19, when they arrive at history's second garden, Peter and John "see" but don't fully realize. Only Mary Magdalene, first among the women who come to anoint a body they expected to find but didn't, is granted sight to behold the risen Christ.

"*Mary.*" As with all his children, Jesus knows this daughter's name, and honors and blesses her faithfulness with his loving call (John 20:11–18).

* * *

20

John Chapter 20

VERSES 1–8

1 On the first day of the week, early in the morning while it was still dark, Mary Magdalene came to the tomb and saw that the stone had been taken away from the tomb.
2 Then she ran and came to Simon Peter and to the other disciple whom Jesus loved and said to them, "They have taken the LORD from the tomb and we do not know where they have laid Him."[1]
3 Then Peter and the other disciple came out and they were going to the tomb.
4 And the two were running together. And the other disciple ran quickly ahead of Peter and came first to the tomb,
5 And stooping over saw the linen cloths lying there, but did not go in.
6 Then Simon Peter came following him and went into the tomb, and saw the linen cloths,

---

1. Even though John names only Mary Magdalene as visiting the tomb, the first person plural form of the verb "we do not know" is significant. Mark 16:1 names as her companions Mary the mother of James and Salome. Matthew 28:1 names "Mary Magdalene and the other Mary," while Luke 24:10 mentions "Mary Magdalene and Joanna and Mary the mother of James and the other women" as those who "told these things" to the apostles (Bernard, *Exegetical Commentary*, 2:656). I believe the Gospel accounts are all consistent, though they do not report events in an identical fashion. For further reading based on this view, see Wenham, *Easter Enigma*, 22–42.

John Chapter 20

7 And the face cloth which had been on His head was not lying with the other cloths but folded up in its own place.[2]

8 Then the other disciple, the one who had come first to the tomb, went in, and saw and believed.

* * *

REFLECTION: SEEING AND BELIEVING

Having reached the tomb first, John now joins Peter, entering and looking inside. But unlike Peter, whose reaction isn't reported in the narrative, John's faith is given sight—he "saw and believed."

Nothing in the account suggests that John sees the risen Christ himself in this moment. But the mere sight of the neatly folded head cloth placed separately from the other burial cloths is enough for John. Even if not fully comprehending all of its ramifications, he believes the miracle of the resurrection, and so also Jesus' identity as Savior-Messiah. Faith truly "becomes sight" for John. He somehow knows and believes in an instant that Jesus is risen indeed! The beloved disciple sees new eternal reality in the early morning light of his divine Rabbi's empty tomb.

Bernard writes of John:

"This was a moment in his inner life, which was so charged with consequence, that he could never forget it, and the incident is recorded here as explaining how and when it was that he reached the fullness of Christian faith. That he 'believed' without 'seeing' his Risen Lord was in marked contrast to the attitude of Thomas, to whom Jesus said, 'Blessed are that they have not seen and yet have believed'" (quoting 20:29).[3]

As a lawyer, I'm trained to be skeptical, trained to pose questions, test alleged "facts" and arguments, look around corners, and assess risk. For me to do so is to protect my clients' interests! By nature I seek "proof." My lawyer's eye has often been a stumbling block in faith matters. Too many times I have either not "seen" (that is, not understood the significance of a spiritual sign given by God) *and* not believed, or have seen but still (for whatever reason) failed to have faith, or only partly believe. John here both sees *and* believes. His is an open heart and active faith.

---

2. These critical forensic details that John includes in the narrative are matter-of-fact in tone but at the same time highly suggestive. Thieves taking the body would hardly have been so neat. The placement of the burial clothes appears as strong evidence for the resurrection.

3. Bernard, *Exegetical Commentary*, 2:661.

> Finally, consider the stone formerly covering the entrance to Christ's tomb. The gospel's witness is that the stone wasn't rolled away to let Jesus *out*. As Lord of and overall creation, Jesus didn't need that. The stone was rolled away to let Mary Magdalene and the disciples *in*—so that they could witness directly with their own eyes the miraculous evidence of Christ's resurrection.
>
> What point of trust is God calling you to see today, and what step of faith is he asking you to take to live into it? Consider, and pray.

* * *

VERSES 9-16

9 For they had not understood the scripture, that He must rise from the dead.[4]

10 Then the disciples departed again to their own [place(s)] where they were staying].

11 But Mary stood outside before the tomb, weeping.[5] As she was weeping, she leaned over [and looked] into the tomb

12 And beheld two angels in white seated, one at the head and the other at the foot of where Jesus' body had lain.

13 And they said to her, "Woman, why do you weep?" She said to them, "They have taken my Lord away and I do not know where they have laid Him."

---

4. John here reminds his readers (almost as if he is saying, "You must remember that") that the disciples did not grasp the scripture that had foretold the resurrection of Christ (Bernard, *Exegetical Commentary*, 2:661). Since John doesn't specify any scripture, we cannot be sure of which one(s) he intends, but one possibility is Hos 6:2 ("on the third day He will raise us up") (Bruce, *Gospel of John*, 386). Others include Ps 16:10, or Isa 53:10–12 (ESV study note).

5. After having been recorded in v. 2 as the original informant of John and Peter about the entrance stone having been rolled away from the tomb and her assumption that Jesus' body had been taken, Mary Magdalene now suddenly reappears in the narrative. Somewhat oddly, no exchange is recorded between either John with his new-found faith, or Peter, and Mary after the disciples emerge from the tomb and return to their homes. Likewise no reason is given for why Mary comes back to the tomb after running into the city to tell the disciples about the tomb's altered condition. Presumably grief along with the desire to find someone who could explain where Jesus' body had been taken, and/or possibly some hope for a new miracle, drive her return.

John Chapter 20

14 Saying these things, she turned behind her and saw Jesus standing there, but she did not realize that it was Jesus.

15 Jesus said to her, "Woman, why do you weep? Who are you seeking?" Thinking it was the gardener she said to him, "Sir, if you have carried Him away, tell me where you have laid Him, and I will take Him away."[6]

16 Jesus said to her, "Mary."

Turning[7] she said to Him in Aramaic, "My Rabbi!" (Rabbi means 'Teacher).

*   *   *

REFLECTION: "MY RABBI!"

Consider this moment in the garden, quiet at sunrise. Mary stands alone before the one whom she calls her Lord, and now realizes it is he, alive.

Mary Magdalene is the first human witness of the Risen Christ's conquest of sin, death, and the devil (2 Cor 5:21 and John 1:29; 1 Cor 15:24–26, 1 Cor 15:54–57; and John 12:31, Col 2:15 and 1 John 3:8).

Jesus honors Mary, whom he had delivered from demon-possession (Luke 8:2), as the first witness to his resurrection. The full implications were surely too great for Mary to grasp all in a single moment. But like the beloved disciple before her, Mary does see and understand. Against all hope, it is Jesus himself, alive, and she declares her love with the simplest of greetings with the honorific "Rabbi!"

If I met Jesus and he called me by name, what would I do? What would you do or say?

*   *   *

---

6. Jesus repeats the angels' question to Mary. In Mary's answer we hear the pathos of her single-minded desire to attend appropriately to the body of her Master. (She apparently does not consider how as a practical matter she would physically be able to move the body to a fitting resting place).

7. "Apparently Mary had turned her face away from Jesus towards the tomb, taking no interest in the [supposed] gardener who gave her no help in her quest; for when she hears her name, she turns round again (στραφεῖσα, *strapheisa*) in amazement. Who is this that calls her 'Mary'? The personal name, addressed to her directly, in well remembered tones, reveals to her in a flash who the speaker is" (Bernard, *Exegetical Commentary*, 2:667).

VERSES 17–31

17 Jesus said to her, "Do not touch Me,[8] for I have not yet ascended to the Father. Go to My brothers and say to them I am going up to My Father and Your Father, to my God and your God."
18 Mary Magdalene went, announcing to the disciples that, "I have seen the Lord" and what He said to her.

19 Then it being evening on that day, the first day of the week, and the doors having been locked where the disciples were on account of fear of the Jews, Jesus came and stood among them and said to them, "Peace be with you."
20 And saying this He showed them His hands and side. Then the disciples rejoiced seeing the Lord.[9]
21 Then Jesus said to them again, "Peace be with you. Just as the Father has sent Me, so also I am sending you."[10]
22 And saying this He breathed on them and said to them, "Receive the Holy Spirit;[11]
23 If you forgive the sins of anyone, they will be forgiven to them; if you withhold forgiveness from anyone, it will be withheld."

---

8. In Matthew's Gospel, Mary Magdalene "and the other Mary" upon seeing Jesus, "came up and took hold of His feet and worshipped Him" (Matt 28:9).

9. The disciples' experience of joy at seeing the resurrected Lord fulfills the promise Jesus made to them in 16:22 ("... I will see you again, and your hearts will rejoice, and no one will take your joy from you") (Bernard, *Exegetical Commentary*, 2:675).

10. "Language of this kind is addressed in the Fourth Gospel to the apostles *alone*; and it is difficult . . . to suppose that in this verse, and here only, the evangelist means us to understand that the great commission was given to all the disciples [as opposed to just the apostles] . . . It is quite just to describe this verse as 'the charter of the Christian Church (Wescott), but the Charter was addressed *in the first instance* to the leaders of the Church, and not to all its members, past and future, without discrimination" (Bernard, *Exegetical Commentary*, 2:676) (emph. added).

11. "Jesus has laid down the principle that 'The Spirit is that which makes alive' (6:63), that is, that the Spirit brings about resurrection. Here the Spirit is both the evidence of resurrection—that is, that Jesus is alive—and the empowerment of the disciples to do what He has just sent them to do" (NICNT). Jesus reprises Genesis for the apostles, enlivening them for his ministry ahead. Recall God "breathing" into Adam's nostrils the breath of life in Gen 2:7, "and man became a living creature." Further, in Ezek 37:9, speaking of the life-giving Spirit of God, "breathe on these slain, that they may live" (see Bernard, *Exegetical Commentary*, 2:677).

John Chapter 20

24 But Thomas one of the Twelve, the one called Didymus[12], was not with them when Jesus came.

25 Then the other disciples were saying to him, "We have seen the LORD." But he said to them, "Unless I see the marks of the nails in His hands and put my hand in His side, I will not believe."

26 And after eight days His disciples were again inside and Thomas was with them. And Jesus came, although the doors were locked, and stood in their midst and said, "Peace be with you."

27 Then He said to Thomas, "Put your finger here and behold My hands, and take your hand and put it in My side, and do not doubt but believe."[13]

28 Thomas answered and said to Him, "My LORD and my God!"[14]

29 Jesus said to him, "You have believed because you have seen me? Blessed are those not seeing and [yet] believing."

30 Jesus indeed did many other signs in the presence of His disciples which are not written in this book.

31 But these are written so that you may believe that Jesus is the Christ, the Son of God,[15] and that believing you may have life in His Name.

---

12. This word in the Greek means "twin."

13. "Jesus offers to Thomas at once the test which he had declared would be essential if he were to credit the story that the Lord had risen, and suggests it in almost the same words that Thomas had used (v. 25). He thus shows to Thomas that he knows what has been in his mind and how he had expressed it. And His words, revealing that this was He who could read men's hearts (2:25), proved sufficient to sweep away all doubt from the mind of His incredulous disciple" (Bernard, *Exegetical Commentary*, 2:682).

14. Ironically, amongst all the disciples, it is Thomas who first voices the knowledge of Jesus for all that He truly is, not just "Teacher" and "Lord" (13:13), but "God." In the doubting disciple's words, we see human faith recognizing at last the "deepest of Christian truths," revealed in the Prologue: "The Word was God . . . The Word became flesh" (1:1, 14). Bernard, *Exegetical Commentary*, 2:683. See also Carson, *According to John*, 659.

15. Note that the form of the Greek verb here is second person plural, i.e., "you all." John is addressing all of his readers across time with this hope and admonition.

21

John Chapter 21

VERSES 1-19

1 After these things Jesus showed Himself again to His disciples beside the Sea of Tiberias. He showed Himself in this way.
2 Simon Peter and Thomas the one called Didymus, Nathaniel from Cana of Galilee, the sons of Zebedee and two other of His disciples were together.
3 Simon Peter said to them, "I'm going fishing."[1] They said to him, "We're going with you." They went and got in the boat, and that night caught nothing.
4 While it was still early in the morning, Jesus stood on the shore, but the disciples didn't know that it was Jesus.
5 Then Jesus said to them, "Children, do you not have any fish?" They answered Him, "No."[2]
6 And He said to them, "Cast the net on the right side of the boat, and you will find some." Then they cast [the net], and weren't able to haul it in because of the multitude of the fish.[3]

---

1. Peter's words suggest the disciples' lives have returned to the *status quo ante* before having encountered Jesus. How prone am I to do likewise, susceptible to the patient seduction of our age and its pervasive idolatry?

2. The disciples' labor after attempting to return to their former lives avails nothing.

3. As in Luke 5:4, Jesus' suggestion results in a plentiful catch for his bedraggled fisher-friends. The Lord takes pity and helps meet his disciples' need for livelihood and sustenance. As usual, Jesus' invitation leads to abundance.

John Chapter 21

7 Then the disciple whom Jesus loved said to Peter, "It is the Lord."[4] Simon Peter hearing that it was the Lord wrapped his garment around himself, for he was naked, and cast himself into the sea,

8 But the other disciples came in the boat, for they were not far from land, about two hundred cubits, dragging the net [full] of fish.[5]

9 Then as they got out on the shore they saw a charcoal fire there with fish laid on it, and bread.[6]

10 Jesus said to them, "Bring some of the fish you have just caught."

11 The Simon Peter got out and hauled the net unto land full of 153 large fish. But even though there were so many, the net was not torn.

12 Jesus said to them, "Come and have breakfast." None of the disciples dared to ask Him, "Who are you?" for they knew that it was the Lord.[7]

13 Jesus came and took the bread and gave it to them, and likewise the fish.

14 This was now the third time that Jesus was revealed[8] to the disciples having been raised from the dead.

---

4. Like Jesus' greeting to Mary ("Mary," 20:16), his grief for Lazarus ("Jesus wept," 11:35) or his powerful promise to Martha ("Your brother will rise again," 11:23), John's simple declaration voices anew the power of Jesus' presence and locates the resurrection in the midst of what until now had been the disciples' again seemingly mundane existence, plying their trade on the Sea of Galilee.

"The Beloved Disciple is the first to recognize Jesus, while Peter is the first to act on the knowledge that the stranger on the shore is He. This is entirely congruous with all that the Gospels tell of the two men, the one a spiritual genius, the other an eager, impulsive, warm-hearted leader" (Bernard, *Exegetical Commentary*, 2:697).

5. A cubit was approximately eighteen inches (ESV), meaning they were about one hundred yards from shore.

6. Jesus provides! As usual, he knows the disciples' need.

7. "Jesus invites them to breakfast as a sense of holy wonder falls upon them. In awestruck silence they eat. They dare not ask, 'who are you?' for the answer can only be "I AM." So they eat what the Lord gives them *and the sharing of the meal is the unveiling of His presence*" (emph. added). Milne, *Message of John*, 311 (quoting Newbigin).

This verse reminds of Luke's testimony of the two disciples' experience on the road to Emmaeus:

> "Then they told what had happened [lit. "the things"] on the road, and how He was known to them in the breaking of the bread" (Luke 24:35).

8. John's use of the passive form of the verb highlights God's agency in the risen Messiah's appearances to his disciples.

15 Then when they had finished Jesus said to Simon Peter, "Simon son of John, do you love me more than these?" He [Peter] said to Him, "Yes Lord, You know that I love You." He [Jesus] said to him, "Feed My lambs."[9]

16 Jesus again said to him a second time, "Simon son of John, do you love Me?" He said to Him, "Yes Lord, You know that I love You." He said to him, "Tend My sheep."

17 He [Jesus] said to him a third time, "Simon son of John, do you love me?"[10] Peter was pained that He had asked him a third time, "Do you love Me?" and said to Him, "Lord, You understand all things, You know that I love You." He said to him, "Feed My sheep.

18 Truly, truly I say to you, when you were young, you dressed yourself and were going where you wished; but when you are old, you will stretch out your hands, and another will dress you and will carry you where you do not wish to go."

19 And He said this to signify by what kind of death he would glorify God. And saying this, He said to him, "Follow Me."[11]

---

9. Jesus' questions make a three-part restoration of Peter, in essence reclaiming from Satan and cancelling once and for all eternity each of Peter's previous three denials of Christ in the hour of the Lord's trial and suffering.

"Jesus' initial question probes Peter to the depth of his being. He does not try to answer in terms of the relative strength of his love as compared with that of other disciples. He appeals rather to the Lord's knowledge. Despite my bitter failure, he says in effect, I love you—*you know that I love you.* Jesus accepts his declaration, doubtless to Peter's relief, and commissions him: *Feed my lambs*" (Carson, *According to John*, 677, orig. emph.).

Separately, certain commentators have tried to adduce significance to alleged distinctions between Jesus' use of the term ἀγαπᾷς με? (*agapas me*) as contrasted with Peter's φιλῶ σε (*philo se*) in the first two questions, However, Bernard (with many scholars) points out that "an analysis of the passages in which these [two Greek verbs 'to love'] occur shows that they are practically synonymous in the Fourth Gospel" (Bernard, *Exegetical Commentary*, 2:702).

10. Here Jesus adopts the verb form Peter has used, mercifully using Peter's own humble language (φιλεῖς με?, *phileis me*) to ask and thereby restore him for the third and final time.

11. "He," that is, Peter. "By the time the Gospel was written, Peter had glorified God in martyrdom" (Bruce, *Gospel of John*, 406). The exact form Peter's martyrdom took isn't clear, though many commentators take Jesus' words to denote crucifixion. Jesus' command to 'follow Me' thus can be read to mean not only follow Me as disciple, but also follow Me in death. In this way, Peter's eager protestation, though deferred, will still be fulfilled: "Lord, I will lay down my life for you" (13:37) (Bruce, *Gospel of John*, 406). More immediately, Jesus' charge here recapitulates his original invitation to Peter and Andrew recorded in the Synoptic Gospels: "Come, and I will make you fishers of men" (Matt 4:19, Mark 1:17; see also Luke 5:10).

John Chapter 21

* * *

REFLECTION: BREAKFAST ON THE SHORE

Thinking of Peter during Holy Week, I'm prone to thinking "I would have never done *that*."

But if I'm honest I recognize there have been countless times and ways in which I've straight-up denied Jesus by thoughts, words, or actions, too many and too shameful to recount. It turns out Peter and I aren't very different, though I confess I've always found it easier to identify with the thief on the Cross who begs Jesus, "Jesus, remember me when You come into Your kingdom" (Luke 23:42).

Going through chemotherapy during Holy Week this year (2023), I've prayed that on the other side of this trial I too could meet Jesus on the shore in the beauty of the morning and that he would likewise fix me a simple, hearty breakfast. Jesus' breakfast would surely be hearty and sufficient!

What shame and pain Peter must have felt, having to turn again into the face of his former denials and humbly confess his love for Jesus. Peter's confession cleanses him as he speaks. (I'm not sure that I would even have had words to answer!) But Jesus is present with him, to hear and receive what Peter confesses, each time, restoring him as he speaks.

The bread and the fish are a simple gift, prepared in love. While not on the physical scale of Jesus' earlier feeding of the five thousand at Passover, this meal is an equally miraculous gift of mercy. Jesus' forgiveness of his chief apostle girds Peter for the work and charge given to him and by extension all of us: "Follow me!"

It's been a long, hard night fishing, with no results to show for it. But Jesus has fixed breakfast, invites me to join Him, and calls me alongside him once more to follow and to serve. God has done His part, now I should do mine, and follow him.

PRAYER

Dearest Jesus, even when I may feel anxious or afraid, or fenced in by health challenges, help me to ever follow you in faith, trusting that you will always provide what's best for me. Grant me eyes to see that, and a heart to trust and abide in your undying love and life. In your blessed name, Amen.

* * *

VERSES 20–25

20 Turning back, Peter saw the disciple whom Jesus loved following, the one who had leaned on His chest at supper and said, "Lord, who is the one betraying you?"
21 Seeing him, Peter said to Jesus, "Lord, what about him?"
22 Jesus said to him, "If I should wish for him to remain until I come, what is that to you? You follow Me."[12]
23 Afterward the word went out amongst the brethren that this disciple would not die; but Jesus did not say to him that he would not die but rather, "If I should wish him to remain until I come, what is that to you?"
24 This disciple is the one testifying to these things and who has written of them,[13] and we know that his testimony is true.
25 And there are also many other things that Jesus did, which if every one was written, I suppose not even the world itself could hold the number of books that would be written.[14]

* * *

SOLI DEO GLORIA

---

12. Jesus gently but firmly reminds Peter to focus on what is to be his key priority for the rest of his days on earth. The Lord is not saying that his will is John will not die, but rather even if that *was* his will, this is no concern of Peter's (Bernard, *Exegetical Commentary*, 2:711).

13. "*Prima facie*, this indicates that Beloved Disciple actually wrote the Gospel with his own hand, including [this] Appendix, and not only that his reminiscences are behind it. But γράφειν (*graphein*) is sometimes used when *dictation* only is intended . . . The employment of scribes was very common . . . This is the meaning which we attach to . . . ["who has written"] in the present passage. The elders of the Church certified that the Beloved Disciple caused these things to be written" (Bernard, *Exegetical Commentary*, 2:713). Whether he personally wrote or dictated this Gospel, this verse clearly attests that the beloved disciple is the author of it.

14. John's closing complements and reminds us of his Gospel's purpose statement in 20:31: ". . . but these are written so that you may believe that Jesus is the Christ, the Son of God, and that by believing you may have life in his name" (ESV).

Appendix

EDITOR'S NOTE

When my father passed away in October 2023 this book was midway through the copyediting process. It fell to me to complete the last steps and I could not have done this without the help of several other people. Since the manuscript had already been submitted, I felt it would be best to thank them in this appendix, which also allows me to explain some of the changes I made and include my father's obituary.

There were several sources and citations that were not listed in the bibliography or missing page numbers, and regarding the correction of these errors I owe special thanks to Rev. Blaise Berg and Mr. Matthew Horwitz of St. Patrick's Seminary & University in Menlo Park, California. My father did not own most of the texts he used when writing this work and had borrowed them from the library at St. Patrick's.

As theological texts like these are not usually available at public libraries, I decided to drive over to St. Patrick's one day to find the missing citations. While I was wandering around campus, Rev. Berg walked by and asked if I needed help. I explained my situation and he very kindly let me use the library for a few hours despite the building being closed and put me in touch with Matthew Horwitz when I realized I would need more time. Mr. Horwitz is the Library Director at St. Patrick's and was very accommodating during my subsequent visits. Without their help, this book would not have been published.

I would also like to thank Dr. William "Chip" Gruen of Muhlenberg College in Allentown, Pennsylvania. I took several of his classes at about the same time my father began his study of Biblical languages, and it was under his tutelage that I learned the basics of Koine Greek. While my knowledge pales in comparison to that of a proper Biblical scholar, the rudimentary

Appendix

command of the language that I acquired during Dr. Gruen's courses has served me well during this project. I also sought his advice regarding the translation of the word κύριος (*kúrios*), as there were some inconsistencies that needed to be resolved. The following explanation is largely drawn from my communications with Dr. Gruen.

Kúrios can be translated four different ways in the New Testament:

1. As a substitute for the personal name of God, also known as the Tetragrammaton. This occurs in quotations from the Old Testament (e.g., John 1:23) and in this book is written using small caps, e.g., "Lord".
2. As a respectful form of address for an adult male, similar "sir" or "mister" in modern English. This occurs when Jesus is being addressed by a nonbeliever, as in John 4:11, or when individuals are addressing one another with respect, as in John 12:21. In this book, this meaning of *kúrios* is translated as, "sir".
3. As in reference to the relationship between a master and a slave or servant, as in John 13:16. In this book, this meaning of *kúrios* is translated as, "master".
4. As a very respectful form of address for an adult male, similar to "sire" or "milord" (rarely used in modern English). This usually occurs when Jesus is being addressed or talked about by a believer, as in John 6:68, and in many translations is written as "lord".

For many instances of *kúrios* that are usually translated as "lord", my father decided to translate it the same way as the Tetragrammaton, i.e., "Lord". I believe this is to imply a very high Christology, or put another way, to highlight the belief on the part of the speakers (the Apostles, Mary Magdalene, etc.) that Jesus was the Son of God. There were also several cases where my father chose to write "lord" where other translations would write "sir" (e.g., John 5:7, 6:34). I believe this is to show a higher level of respect than "sir" without implying that the speaker is a believer.

There are a few cases where I have elected to change my father's original translation. While I believe some of these were simple errors on, the more substantive changes I made are as follows:

- John 8:11, where Jesus saves the adulteress from stoning. Whereas many translations have "sir", my father translated it as "Lord", thus implying that the adulteress believes Jesus is Son of God. I do not think that there is enough in the text to speak to the adulteress' belief, but

Appendix

I am sure she was grateful to Jesus for saving her life and may have been aware of Jesus' reputation as a teacher. I elected to translate this instance of *kúrios* as "lord".

- John 9:36, where Jesus heals the blind man. Many translations have the blind man addressing Jesus as "sir", but my father chose to translate it as "Lord". This appears to be an error, as in 9:39 the blind man says, "Lord, I believe", which would imply that up until 9:39 he does not believe that Jesus is the Son of God. I think it makes more sense to translate 9:36 as "lord" to convey the blind man's gratitude for being healed and to keep in line with his statement that Jesus was a prophet in 9:17.

I am sure my father will let me know if I got it right when I see him again.

There were a variety of smaller errors scattered throughout the manuscript that were discovered later in the editing process (capitalizations, missing parentheses, etc.). I endeavored to leave as much of the original text unchanged as possible, and when in doubt I adopted the style of the English Standard Version, which was my father's preferred translation of the Bible.

While his illness weighed heavily on him during his final months, I know that my father took great comfort in God's word and the good news contained therein. I hope this book has the same effect on you.

Joseph A. H. Comey

APPENDIX

OBITUARY

Charles Christopher Comey passed away at the age of 61 on October 9, 2023, in Palo Alto, California. He is survived by his wife, Judith Huang, and his three sons, Joseph, Franklin, and Ian.

Chuck, as his friends called him, was born in Cleveland, Ohio on April 6, 1962, to Ralph Howard Comey Jr. and Jacqueline Jessie Comey (née Jones). In 1972 the family moved to Tucson, Arizona, where Chuck graduated from Rincon High School in 1980. In 1984 he obtained a B.A. in English from Yale University (*cum laude*).

He traveled to China through the Yale-China Association to teach English for a year in Zhenjiang, Jiangsu Province, thus beginning a lifelong association with China. He then obtained an M.A. in East Asian Studies from the University of California, Berkeley in 1987. While studying Chinese at the Stanford Center at National Taiwan University in Taipei, he met his future wife, Judith. They got married on December 26, 1989.

Chuck then studied law at the University of California, Los Angeles, obtaining his J.D. in 1991. Later that year he joined the Palo Alto office of Morrison & Foerster. He would spend the rest of his 32-year legal career at this firm specializing in cross-border mergers and acquisitions. At the same time, he also began his involvement in church leadership, becoming a deacon at the Chinese Church in Christ in Mountain View.

Appendix

In 1994, shortly after the birth of his son Joseph, the family moved to Japan, where Chuck worked at the Tokyo office for nine years. During this time, he served as an elder at Tokyo Baptist Church and welcomed two more sons, Franklin and Ian.

The family then moved to Shanghai, China, where Chuck opened Morrison & Foerster's Shanghai office and served as managing partner for seven years. He also served as chairman of the Board of Elders for Abundant Grace International Fellowship in Shanghai until the family returned to the U.S. in 2010. In 2019 he obtained an M.A. in Theology from Fuller Theological Seminary with an emphasis in ethics and Biblical languages, despite battling lung cancer.

Chuck was a strong, intelligent, and generous man, with a deep love for his family and for God. He was fiercely loyal, honest to a fault, and set a high moral standard for himself and those around him. He will be greatly missed by friends and family alike.

Bibliography

Aland, Kurt, et al., eds. *The Greek New Testament*. 5th Revised. Stuttgart: Deutsche Bibelgeselleschaft, 2014.
Arnette, Jeff. "The Seven Feasts in John's Gospel." https://centralhaywoodcoc.com/2019/06/16/the-seven-feasts-in-johns-gospel/.
Bernard, J. H. *A Critical and Exegetical Commentary on the Gospel According to St. John*. Edited by A. H. McNeile. 2 vols. International Critical Commentary on the Holy Scriptures of the Old and New Testaments 29. New York: Scribner's, 1929.
Bible Atlas. "Arimathea." https://bibleatlas.org/full/arimathea.htm.
BibleProject. "BibleProject." https://bibleproject.com/.
———. "John 1–12." https://bibleproject.com/explore/video/john-1-12/.
———. "The Significance of Seven." https://bibleproject.com/podcast/significance-7/.
Bouyer, Louis. *The Meaning of Sacred Scripture*. Notre Dame: University of Notre Dame Press, 1958.
Brown, Raymond E. *The Gospel According to John, XIII–XXI*. Garden City, NY: Doubleday & Company, 1970.
Bruce, F. F. *The Gospel of John*. Grand Rapids: Eerdmans, 1983.
Brunson, Andrew. "Don't Be Offended by Christ." *Decision*, Jul/Aug, 2002. 29-30.
Carson, D. A. *The Gospel According to John*. Grand Rapids: Eerdmanns, 1992.
Coffman, James Burton. "Coffman's Commentaries on the Bible - John 8." https://www.studylight.org/commentaries/eng/bcc/john-8.html.
Cyril of Alexandria. *Commentary on John*. Translated by David R. Maxwell, edited by Joel C. Elowsky. 2 vols. Downers Grove, IL: InterVarsity, 2015.
Daily Dose of Greek. "Daily Dose of Greek." https://dailydoseofgreek.com/.
Danker, Frederick William, ed. *A Greek-English Lexicon of the New Testament and Other Early Christian Literature*. Chicago: University of Chicago Press, 2000.
Donne, John. *The Poems of John Donne*, edited by Herbert J. C. Grierson. 1st ed. London: Oxford University Press, 1912.
Ellis, E. Earle. *The World of St. John: St. John's Gospel and the Epistles*. New York: Abingdon, 1965.
Encyclopedia Britannica. "Exegesis." https://www.britannica.com/topic/exegesis.
Esolen, Anthony. *In the Beginning Was the Word: An Annotated Reading of the Prologue of John*. Brooklyn: Angelico, 2021.
Fee, Gordon D., and Douglas Stuart. *How to Read the Bible Book by Book: A Guided Tour*. Grand Rapids: Zondervan, 2002.

Bibliography

Guthrie, Donald, et. al., eds. *The New Bible Commentary Revised*. London: InterVarsity, 1970.

Henry, Matthew. *Matthew Henry's Commentary on the Whole Bible*. Grand Rapids: Zondervan, 1961.

Laden, Jonathan. "The Royal Purple of David and Solomon." https://www.biblicalarchaeology.org/daily/biblical-artifacts/artifacts-and-the-bible/the-royal-purple-of-david-and-solomon/.

Lyte, Henry Francis. "419. Abide with Me." https://hymnary.org/hymn/HWC1986/419.

Metzger, Bruce, ed. *A Textual Commentary on the Greek New Testament*. 2nd ed. Stuttgart: Deutsche Bibelgesellschaft, 1996.

Milne, Bruce. *The Message of John*. Downers Grove, IL: InterVarsity, 1993.

Oden, Thomas, ed. *Ancient Christian Commentary on Scripture Updated Version*. 2019.

Poole, Matthew. "A Commentary on the Holy Bible." https://www.studylight.org/commentaries/eng/mpc/john-1.html.

Robertson, A. T. *Word Pictures in the New Testament*. 6 vols. Nashville: Broadman, 1930–33.

Schaff, Philip, and Henry Wace, eds. *Nicene and Post-Nicene Fathers: Second Series*. 14 vols. Peabody: Hendrickson, 1995.

Stefon, Matt. "Dao." https://www.britannica.com/topic/dao.

Stonehouse, Ned, et al., eds. *The New International Commentary on the New Testament*. Grand Rapids: Eerdmans, 2007.

Tasker, R. V. G. *John*. Leicester: Inter-University Press, 2000.

Van Pelt, Miles V., and Gary D. Pratico. *Graded Reader of Biblical Hebrew: A Guide to Reading the Hebrew Bible*. Grand Rapids: Zondervan Academic, 2006.

Wellman, Jack. "What Does the Number Twelve (12) Mean or Represent in the Bible?" https://www.patheos.com/blogs/christiancrier/2014/09/28/what-does-the-number-twelve-12-mean-or-represent-in-the-bible/.

Wenham, John. *Easter Enigma: Are the Resurrection Accounts in Conflict?* Milton Keynes, UK: Paternoster, 1992.

Wikipedia. "Docetism." https://en.wikipedia.org/wiki/Docetism.

———. "Pilate's Court." https://en.wikipedia.org/wiki/Pilate%27s_court.

———. "Samaritan Pentateuch." https://en.wikipedia.org/wiki/Samaritan_Pentateuch.

www.ingramcontent.com/pod-product-compliance
Lightning Source LLC
Chambersburg PA
CBHW051936160426
43198CB00013B/2176